Praise for *How to Save Your Child from Ostrich
Attacks, Accidental Time Travel, and Anything Else
That Might Happen on an Average Tuesday*

"Not worried about random ostrich attacks? Maybe you should be. All the
good parents are reading *How to Save Your Child*. You do want to be a good
parent, don't you? James Breakwell is brilliant, funny, hilarious, and possibly
someone you'd want to have nearby in cases of ostrich attacks and accidental
time travel, but what you definitely want to have around is his new book,
which is a hysterical, survivable romp through this mad world."
—Carrie Jones, *New York Times* bestselling author of *Need*

"I adore this book, which, by the way, all parents should read for a laugh or
just to realize you're not alone in the insanity."
—Jill Shalvis, *New York Times* bestselling
author of *The Lucky Harbor series*

"Nonstop, laugh-out-loud wit sprinkled with shockingly insightful parenting truths. Literally, no other parenting book has the courage to address
accidental time travel. Bravo."
—Joel Willis, executive editor of *The Dad*

"James has done it again with another hilarious book that manages to be
completely off-the-wall and entirely relatable at the same time! Thanks
to James's book, I'm prepared for any situation and several steps closer to
immortality."
—Hal Lublin, voiceover actor and host of the
podcast *We Got This with Mark and Hal*

Praise for *Only Dead on the Inside*

"The quintessential guide on the topic. It will make you laugh; it will make you think; it will make you wonder the barter value of your children in case things get crazy. You need this book if you wanna live."
—Kevin Sussman, actor on the hit CBS sitcom *The Big Bang Theory*

"I have to admit: I giggled."
—Jessica Lahey, *New York Times* bestselling author of *The Gift of Failure*

"At first I was like, 'Oh, great, another hilarious parenting book written by a viral internet sensation. Just what the world doesn't need.' But then I finally read *Only Dead on the Inside* and realized this was a hilarious parenting book by a viral internet sensation *with zombies* and I was like, 'I was wrong. The world does need this!' You'll chortle, you'll chuckle, and you might even learn something."
—Jen Mann, *New York Times* bestselling author of *People I Want to Punch in the Throat: Competitive Crafters, Drop-Off Despots, and Other Suburban Scourges*

"This guide to parenting through the apocalypse is so darkly hilarious, you don't even need to be a parent or have experienced an apocalypse to enjoy it."
—Liz Climo, artist for *The Simpsons*, author, and creator of viral comics on lizclimo.tumblr.com

"Are you a parent of cute, selfish, tiny people who look like you but don't pay rent, destroy your sleep, inspire homicidal thoughts, and shatter your self-confidence daily? Do you need help to survive this crisis? (Yes, yes you do.) Long-suffering parent, you must immediately read James Breakwell's hilarious, fast-paced, and practical book chock-full of wisdom, to-do lists, rules, and big pie charts and graphs. Breakwell not only taught me how to survive the madness of parenthood, but also how to protect my babies from becoming undead, crawling, brain-eating monsters in diapers after the inevitable zombie apocalypse."

—Wajahat Ali, speaker and *New York Times* op-ed contributor

Praise for *Bare Minimum Parenting*

"A painfully honest and hilarious parenting book for us non-parenting-book-reading underachievers trying to survive the whole parenting experience. You know, I really could have used this book before my kids drove me insane. Next time write faster, James."

—Brian Gordon, creator of the webcomic *Fowl Language*

"James Breakwell's *Bare Minimum Parenting: The Ultimate Guide to Not Quite Ruining Your Child* is a witty and refreshing take on parenting in a modern world. I have always enjoyed following James' parental trials and tribulations on social media, and it's fun seeing his musings come to life in this essential handbook!"

—Rebecca Mader, actress in *Once Upon a Time* and *Lost*

"I've never felt so guilt-free ignoring my child to read a book."

—Laura Perlongo, Shorty Award–winning cohost of the web series *We Need to Talk* and guest commentator on MTV's *Catfish*

"Breakwell has a hit . . . uproariously funny and, at times, unexpectedly poignant."

—Liliana Hart, *New York Times* bestselling author and mom of five

HOW ⬚TO⬚ SAVE YOUR CHILD

⬚FROM⬚

OSTRICH ATTACKS, ACCIDENTAL TIME TRAVEL, AND ANYTHING ELSE THAT MIGHT HAPPEN ON AN AVERAGE TUESDAY

**Other Titles by
James Breakwell**

*Only Dead on the Inside
Bare Minimum Parenting
Prance Like No One's Watching*

HOW [TO] SAVE YOUR CHILD

[FROM]

OSTRICH ATTACKS, ACCIDENTAL TIME TRAVEL,

AND ANYTHING ELSE THAT MIGHT HAPPEN ON AN AVERAGE TUESDAY

JAMES BREAKWELL

BENBELLA

BenBella Books, Inc.
Dallas, TX

BenBella

BenBella Books, Inc.
10440 N. Central Expressway, Suite 800
Dallas, TX 75231
www.benbellabooks.com
Send feedback to feedback@benbellabooks.com

Printed in the United States of America
10 9 8 7 6 5 4 3 2 1

Library of Congress Control Number: 2019016955.
ISBN 9781948836456 (trade paper)
ISBN 9781948836708 (electronic)

Editing by Leah Wilson
Copyediting by James Fraleigh
Proofreading by Lisa Story and Michael Fedison
Text design and composition by Aaron Edmiston
Cover design by Sarah Avinger
Cover and interior illustrations by James Breakwell
Printed by Versa Press

Distributed to the trade by Two Rivers Distribution, an Ingram brand
www.tworiversdistribution.com

Special discounts for bulk sales are available.
Please contact bulkorders@benbellabooks.com.

To cheese. No particular reason.
It just doesn't get thanked enough.

CONTENTS

CHAPTER 1

HOW TO SURVIVE ANYTHING

Wake up. Get the kids dressed. Fight off a great white shark. Make breakfast. Get thrown back in time to the Cretaceous period. Bills.

If you're a parent, that sounds like a normal weekday morning. If you're a nonparent, it sounds like you should double-check your birth control. Nothing is more terrifying to the childless than an honest look at what it's like to raise a kid. The struggle is real.

For some parts of that struggle, I'm no help at all. I have no idea how you're supposed to wake up in the morning, especially since shrill beeps are powerless against parent-level exhaustion and my prototype electric-shock alarm clock was banned for being "dangerous and unethical." Thanks for nothing, FDA.

But for shark attacks and accidental time travel, I have the answers. Life is full of deadly challenges that, to nonparents, seem absurd and unlikely, but to veteran moms and dads, are just an average Tuesday. Or Wednesday, Thursday, or Friday. Quite frankly, there are no safe days when you have a child, mainly because of your child. The greatest threat is right next to you all the time.

That's why I wrote this book. It walks you through practical, real-world survival scenarios like battling ghosts, living out the plot of *Super Mario Bros.*, and fending off an invasion of killer robots. As a parent, you're tough enough to survive all those things. If you made it through that time your toddler threw up at the drive-thru when you were an hour from home and you forgot the diaper bag, you can handle a disembodied spirit or two. You just need a little guidance.

Keep in mind all of this advice is based on carefully researched scientific data I made up off the top of my head. But I assume my guide works because no one has come back to tell me it doesn't. Anyone who found out firsthand that it failed them is already dead. And that's why you can never trust the review section.

But you can trust me because I've dabbled in the insanely dangerous challenges of parenting a few times before. In my first book, *Only Dead on the Inside: A Parent's Guide to Surviving the Zombie Apocalypse*, I tackled the question of

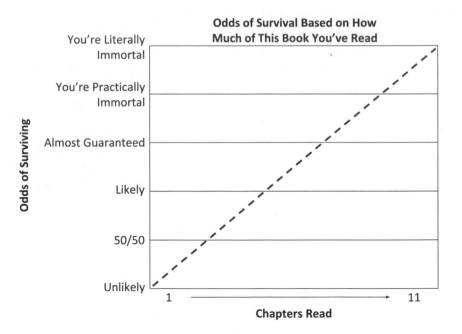

how to raise a normal, loving family when the world is overrun by the undead. That's way more practical than *What to Expect When You're Expecting*. In my second book, *Bare Minimum Parenting: The Ultimate Guide to Not Quite Ruining Your Child*, I addressed how to deal with overachieving parents, who are less gory than the undead but twice as annoying. Give me zombies any day. All of the research I did for those books—also none—gave me the experience and credibility I needed to take on every other parenting challenge on the face of the earth. And occasionally underwater or in outer space. This book goes everywhere. It's amazing how far willful ignorance will take you.

As you go through this book, take everything I say as literally as possible, especially the stuff that contradicts all the other stuff. No one disagrees with me more than me. If you want to live, you have to follow all of it. The stakes are high, except in the case of vampire attacks, where the stakes should be kept at chest level. Try not to be blinded by their sparkles. Vampires are the real reason Corey Hart wears his sunglasses at night.

People Who Should Read This Book

Person	Why They Should Read It
Stay-at-Home Parent	There's no place more dangerous than the home.
Parent Who Works Outside the Home	There's no place more dangerous than the outside world.
Absentee Parent	There's nothing more dangerous than being away from your kid.
Helicopter Parent	There's nothing more dangerous than being too close to your kid.
Lawn-Mower Parent	There's nothing more dangerous than a poorly maintained lawn.
Jetpack Parent	There's nothing more dangerous than being cooler than all the other parents.

Person	Why They Should Read It
Any Other Kind of Parent	There's nothing more dangerous than having a kid.
Nonparent	There's nothing more dangerous than other people's kids.

Don't feel like you have to read this book straight through. Jump to whatever section you need right now. If you and your kid are currently being attacked by a polar bear, by all means skip ahead to the polar bear section. Or maybe go to some other section, because when you're being eaten by a polar bear, the last thing you want to read about is more of the same. The section on sentient furniture might be a nice break.

Sometimes, it might seem like this book is more of a parenting guide than a survival manual. Other times, it might seem like this is just a regular survival guide with kids tacked on because, as a pigeonholed parenting comedy writer, that's all I'm allowed to write about. Shhh. I won't tell anyone if you don't.

As you go about the thankless job of keeping yourself and your child alive, keep these dos and don'ts in mind:

✓ **Do** expect death around every corner. Stick to round rooms and never-ending hallways.

✗ **Don't** be afraid to be a pessimist. If you have to be dead, you might as well also be right.

✓ **Do** keep an eye on your child at all times. Maybe two eyes. Three or more eyes might be overkill as well as anatomically challenging.

✗ **Don't** expect your kid to help out at all. They always assume they're safe. And maybe they are, but only because you're constantly terrified enough for both of you.

✓ **Do** trust your instincts. The only reason you're alive today is because all your ancestors were just as afraid as you are.

✗ **Don't** put this book down. You'll really kick yourself if the one day you and your kid get thrown back in time to the Hundred Years' War is the day you left this book on your nightstand.

✓ **Do** buy more than one copy of this book. Fending off mortal peril by land, sea, and space is hard on book bindings. Be prepared with several backup copies.

✗ **Don't** fact-check this book. Other sources will disagree with me on everything I say. Those sources are wrong.

With a little reading and a lot of luck, you and your child just might survive the slings and arrows life throws your way. Honestly, slings and arrows are pretty easy to survive when thrown. It's when they're shot at high velocity that they cause problems. This book will help you make it through all kinds of dangers like that, but not exactly that, since I wrote the introduction last and the chapter on slings and arrows didn't make the cut. So if an arrow is headed for you right now, hold up this book to block it. And then pull out your backup book to read chapter two.

CHAPTER 2

WILD ANIMALS

There's a reason animals and children seem like they have a special bond: They're basically the same thing. They're both wild, dangerous, and resistant to hygiene. But just because your child acts and smells like other animals doesn't mean your kid will be safe from them. Many animals are capable of killing prey moments after they leave the womb, while your child will be functionally useless until their early thirties. Thanks, extended adolescence. If you want to keep your kid alive (if you don't, you're reading the wrong book), you'll have your work cut out for you. Hopefully that work won't include literally cutting out your child. That's bad for your kid, bad for the animal that swallowed them, and bad for your good scissors.

BEARS

Let's talk about bears—but not too loudly or they'll hear us. Even words in your head should be a whisper. Bears have some of the most finely tuned ears in the animal kingdom. A grizzly can hear you open a bag of chips thirty miles away. So half the distance your kid can.

Bears are nature's perfect killing machines. You can't outrun them, you can't out-climb them, and you can't beat them at karaoke, even if "Livin' on a Prayer" is totally your song after a few drinks. The only place safe from bears is the vacuum of space, and even there, water bears can survive indefinitely. Yes, water bears are microscopic organisms that have no relation to bears other than sharing a name, but it's only a matter of time until they evolve teeth and start attacking astronauts. The International Space Station better secure its trash can.

So how are you supposed to survive these unstoppable killing machines yourself, let alone protect your kid? It all comes down to motivation—theirs, not yours. Bears are the second laziest creatures on earth. The laziest, of course, are human children. It's been an hour, and my seven-year-old still can't find the motivation to put on her second sock. But bears sleep months at a time by design, and everyone just leaves them alone. Can you imagine any other animal spending that much time unconscious and NOT being eaten by something else? Bears rose to the top of the food chain solely so they could dedicate half their lives to sleep. It's the world's most intimidating power nap.

Bears usually attack humans only when their offspring are threatened. Think of all the crazy things you would do to protect your kid. You know, like standing up to an attacking bear. And that's where we hit an impasse.

To stop a bear attack, remind the attacking mama or papa bear that you're an exhausted parent just like them. Complain about your child, preferably in a loud voice so your kid can hear you. That way, if the bear eats you, your kid will remember all the mean things you said and run away to save themselves, rather than trying to save your life, because screw you.

But it's also possible that when the bear hears you complaining, it will stop charging and instead complain about its own kids. You won't speak each other's languages, but context clues will say it all: the howls, the missing hair, the animalistic sense of defeat. And that's just from you.

After you bond over how miserable your kids make you, you and the bear will go your separate ways. Or better yet, you'll become best friends. Invite the bear to your next parent-group meeting. You'll finally have the backup you always wanted. Let's see one of those snooty super-parents shame you in front of a fifteen-hundred-pound Kodiak. You and your new-found bear friend can do anything together. The sky is the limit because

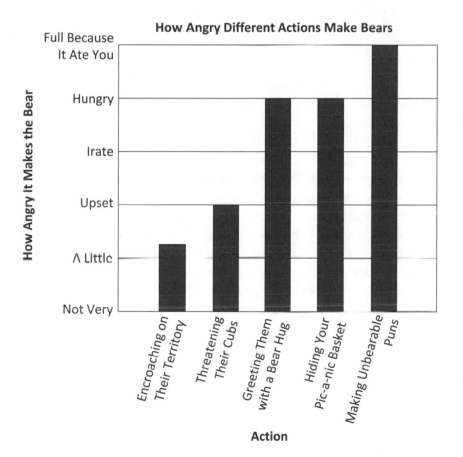

bears can go literally anywhere, including the sky. It's a small step from riding a circus unicycle to piloting an F-16. Welcome to the Bear Force.

Of course, these tips only work for brown and black bears. Polar bears won't bond with you over mutual whining. They'll just kill you and your child as quickly as possible so they can get back to their den. It's too cold outside to make friends.

To keep your kid safe from polar bears in the Arctic Circle, don't take your kid to the Arctic Circle. Seriously, what kind of vacation is that? There are no major theme parks, and Santa's workshop is just one big tourist trap. Try Hawaii instead.

PANDA BEARS

Officially, panda bears are harmless, cuddly animals who would never hurt a fly. Unofficially, pandas are killing machines in cuter outfits.

Pandas kill people all the time, but family members of the victims cover it up. They usually make up some less-embarrassing cause of death, like autoerotic asphyxiation. Never trust a death certificate.

Make no mistake: Panda bears are an extreme threat to your child. These black-and-white animals look innocent and adorable, so your kid is more likely to walk up to one. Why would a panda attack your kid? Maybe your kid smells like food. You just had to install those bamboo floors. It's also possible you came across the panda on a bad day or your kid is just super annoying. I've seen gerbils attack kids, and those aren't exactly man-eaters. Children bring out the worst in everyone.

At least your kid will see the panda attack coming. Pandas are terrible at everything, including camouflage—unless they're hiding in a tuxedo shop. Approach your tailor with caution. Also, pandas aren't particularly fast or motivated, so your kid would pretty much have to walk right up to one and smack it in the face to set off an attack. Naturally, that's exactly what your kid will do.

To save your kid from a vicious panda attack, pick up your child and move them a few steps away. The panda will immediately lose interest. That's why pandas evolved to be herbivores. They only want food that can't run away.

We could prevent all panda attacks on children by letting pandas go extinct. They clearly want to. They have a super-low sex drive, only have one baby at a time, and often reject that baby for no reason. In fact, they're so unfit for survival that not surviving became their survival strategy. Pandas refused to do anything to avoid dying out, so humans stepped in to breed them in captivity. Now people feed them, artificially inseminate them, and raise their offspring for them. Pandas might be the smartest animals ever to live. Forget about saving your child's life. Keep your kid away from panda enclosures simply so they don't pick up some bad habits. There's no coming back from that level of lazy.

BOA CONSTRICTORS

It's easy for a boa constrictor to sneak up on you and your kid. Snakes don't have legs, so you won't hear footsteps. And they don't growl, roar, or make awkward small talk you might overhear. They're like ninjas that wiggle around on their bellies. If that doesn't give you nightmares, it's only because the fear of boa constrictors makes it impossible to sleep.

Boa constrictors kill their prey by squeezing it. It's basically death by hug. To prepare your kid to defend against that, hug your child frequently, ideally at embarrassing times. For your kid, that's basically always. As your child frantically tries to wiggle out of your arms, they'll exercise a powerful, innate survival instinct. Nobody fights off your affection like your own offspring.

If all that practice writhing doesn't help your child escape the boa, drop your kid and the snake around them in a bathtub of water that isn't exactly the right temperature. Whether it's slightly too hot or a touch too cold, wild thrashing will ensue. Your kid will either knock off the snake outright or get enough breathing room to scream—but not about being slowly squeezed to death. All your child's concerns will be strictly bathwater related. You're a terrible parent due to your poor water temperature control, and your kid wants people in the next state to know it.

Luckily, boa constructors aren't used to a lot of noise. Asphyxiation tends to be rather quiet. When your kid screams at the top of their lungs, it will shock the snake. Boa constrictors aren't built to tolerate the kind of shrill noises that confuse sonars and make submarines run aground. At that close range, your child's entire high-pitched tantrum will be funneled directly into the snake's tiny brain. If the boa constrictor doesn't immediately release your kid and slither away, its head will explode. Either way, this will leave you to deal with your child's tantrum, which is worse than any snake attack. Maybe if you're really nice, the boa constrictor will come back and swallow you instead. A parent can dream.

Types of Dangerous Snakes

Type of Snake	Why It's Dangerous
Garter Snake	Hides around a bride's leg
Cape Cobra	Can fly like Superman
Spitting Cobra	Chews tobacco
King Cobra	Pent-up male aggression due to lack of queen cobras
Black Mamba	Will out-dance you, even without legs
Water Moccasin	More poisonous than leather moccasins
Timber Rattlesnake	Knows a tree is falling, but won't warn you
Anaconda	Doesn't want none unless you've got buns, hun

BUTTERFLIES

Butterflies are surprisingly deadly to children. The monarch butterfly is poisonous if eaten. Why would a child eat a butterfly? Stupid question. Kids will eat anything—except what you want them to eat.

Other butterfly species are deadly in subtler ways. Your child could chase a butterfly into traffic or off a cliff. Or, worse, your child might open their mouth in awe of the butterfly's beautiful colors and then the butterfly could fly down their windpipe and make them choke to death. That might seem unlikely, but a torpedo once flew down a vent shaft to blow up the Death Star. All things are possible with the Force.

So how can you protect your child from a vicious butterfly attack? The first step is to recognize an attack is underway. Since butterflies don't really attack, this could be tricky. Ask yourself if your child is paying attention to a butterfly. If the answer is affirmative, ask yourself if that butterfly has sinister intentions. The answer is always yes. The only good butterfly is a dead butterfly. Actually, that's not true. A dead monarch butterfly is just as poisonous as a live one. The only good butterfly is one you thought was a butterfly but was actually just a leaf or something. Crush it anyway just to be safe.

To protect your child from butterflies, you could chase away every butterfly yourself. Unfortunately, that would make you vulnerable to distractedly stepping in front of a moving vehicle. Butterfly-related traffic deaths have no age limit.

Alternatively, you could train your child to ignore butterflies. This seems unlikely. Butterflies are designed specifically to attract attention. They even have an inspirational backstory where they start out as lowly caterpillars and transform themselves into beautiful flutter fairies. Viewed more accurately, they transform themselves from harmless wooly worms into child-killing murder bugs. The children's classic *The Very Hungry Caterpillar* is actually a horror story.

Your best bet to keep your child safe is to move someplace too cold for butterflies to survive. Canada is a nice choice, but rumor has it that it thaws out a few weeks per year. In that brief window, butterfly-related fatalities skyrocket. Of course, the official numbers never reflect that reality because statisticians are under the sway of the powerful butterfly lobby. That's why tourism brochures portray butterflies as a local attraction rather than a serious health hazard on par with dysentery or cholera. Killer butterflies are big business.

I won't advocate killing butterflies to protect your child. For liability purposes, it's dangerous to advocate killing anything in a book, even if that book is the perfect size and weight for smashing butterflies. Besides, the butterflies might seek revenge against me. If I ever die under mysterious circumstances, it was the butterflies. Or a lifetime of poor lifestyle choices. Either way, avenge my death.

But you don't have to destroy butterflies to avoid these dangers. If you and your child can't relocate to a colder climate, stock up on butterfly nets. You can scoop up the butterflies and harmlessly release them someplace they won't cause as much damage, at least to you. Consider releasing them in enemy territory. The US government could save millions on drone strikes if it embraced a butterfly catch-and-release program. It might not be the fastest military strategy, but it would be the prettiest. Those bright colors will really make the battlefield pop.

GEESE

After creating the earth and everything on it, God rested. During that nap, Satan snuck in and created geese. These demonic fowl possess exactly the right mix of hatred and stupidity to make them a threat to all living things, including your child. Geese attack anything and everything because they're too dumb not to, and we let them get away with it because we don't want to cause a scene. Social propriety will be the death of us all. That's what happened to the Neanderthals.

The taboo on fighting back against geese is hard to break. To the untrained observer, geese appear harmless. If you get attacked by one and defend yourself, you'll look like a jerk, and if you mount a preemptive strike, you'll look like a monster. Geese perpetuate their façade of innocence by crossing the road trailed by long lines of adorable baby geese, earning them sympathy even as they halt traffic and bring local commerce to a standstill. But remember, these geese aren't relocating to a better place to raise their goslings. They're marching their feathered demon spawn off to war.

A goose's unnaturally long neck puts it at eye-level with your child, making its painful beak bites that much more damaging. A goose is basically a mean turkey with a head mounted on a feathered snake. Geese can trap you and your child inside your house, forcing you to deal with a cooped-up kid full of unspent energy. Even when the geese fly off to terrorize someone else, they leave behind fields of poop that make your yard unusable for months. This is nothing less than avian terrorism. Enough is enough.

Even if you manage to escape the house and take your child to the park, your luck won't be any better. Geese have no more respect for public property than they do for private. They think every park is their exclusive breeding ground, and woe to you and your child if you disagree. Your kid will be met with a whirlwind of wings, beaks, and honking the likes of which they have never seen. With such a strong defense, geese are free to spawn generation after generation of evil from their mobile hatcheries. What's a parent to do?

To stop a goose, you have to think like a goose. Or rather, not think like a goose. Their minds are completely blank, so yours should be, too. When a goose charges your child, jump in front of your kid without giving it a second thought—or a first thought. Now you're on an equal playing field. The goose will no doubt expect you to flee as it honks and tries to bite you. Stand your ground. The goose is used to bullying smarter creatures that know it isn't worth the fight. But in your current form, you know nothing. The goose has met its match.

When the goose honks, honk back. When it bites, bite back. This will be a challenge because your head isn't mounted on the end of a prehensile hose. If you do make contact with your teeth, you won't hurt the goose (it's too stupid to feel pain, and its down feathers work as an added layer of armor against your incisors), but you will annoy it. While your bites will be individually ineffective, your constant, unrelenting attacks will pester the goose into submission. This tactic should sound familiar. Your kid uses it on you every day.

Ideally, the goose will give up and fly away. But even if you die from goose bites before that strategic retreat, you still win. Your death will show geese everywhere that the human race is done being pushed around by flying Christmas dinners. Of course, geese are too stupid to remember this lesson. Your death will be meaningless. But at least your kid will get a few extra joyless minutes on the monkey bars before the geese chase them away for good. That's parenting well done.

Alternatively, you could skip trying to bite the goose at all and instead throw ice cubes at it. The goose will think it's winter and migrate south, making it somebody else's problem. If you live in the South, I recommend moving North. We'll divide America in half, with warm, swampy regions left to the birds and the temperate north reserved for us. There would be a generous demilitarized zone between the two, and geese and humans would finally have peace. Of course, geese are too stupid to respect treaties, so people would have to walk around with ice cubes in their pockets anyway, just in case. It will be a literal cold war. Keep your throwing mittens handy.

What Groups of Animals Are Called

Animal	What a Group of Them Is Called
Lion	A pride
Crow	A murder
Goose	A flying poo storm
Clown	A nightmare
Bigfoot	A Bigfeet
Adult	A meeting
Politician	A corruption
Child	A mistake

OSTRICHES

You're sitting in your breakfast nook, sipping a warm beverage and helping your kid with their homework, when suddenly an enraged ostrich kicks in your front door. That's Wednesday for you. Here's what to do.

First, accept that this is a plausible scenario you need to plan for. There's no point in sitting there in denial as an agitated ostrich murders your family. Ostriches, like geese, are too stupid to experience mercy or remorse. Also, their knees bend backward, which is unsettling. As the ostrich kicks you to death, you won't even be able to think of your loved ones because you'll be too fixated on those weird knees. What a terrible way to die.

I once met an ostrich farmer, and he acted like he was just trying to make a living, not spreading a plague of long-necked kill storks. Yeah, right. But he did give me one potentially lifesaving tip: If an ostrich attacks you, hold a broom over your head, bristles up. Then the ostrich will think you're an even bigger ostrich and respect you, at least as far as ostriches are capable of respect. That basically means they'll stop kicking you, at least as long as your arm strength holds up. If you ever set down the broom, though, you're going to die. Hope you're okay having dusty floors for the rest of your life.

I disagree with the broom tactic. Even if your biceps are strong enough to hold up a broom indefinitely, dominance has its drawbacks. By becoming the alpha ostrich, you'll take upon yourself the mantle of ostrich leadership. Do you want to lead the annual Ostrich Day Parade or administer ostrich affairs of state? There aren't enough hours in a day to both lead the ostriches and raise your kid. If only there were some way to defeat an ostrich that didn't involve assuming a hereditary leadership position for life.

But wait, there is: ostrich punching. In their entire evolutionary history, ostriches have never had to deal with a swift punch to the gut. I'm not even sure where an ostrich's gut is. Maybe in the front? It doesn't matter. It's not a tactic predators use, so it's not something ostriches know how to defend against. Punch away at whatever you can reach. An ostrich has weak bird bones. At least I assume it does. Full disclosure: I've never punched an ostrich. If you do hit one, let me know how it goes. If it doesn't work, it's because you're a bad puncher, not because I gave you bad advice.

But what should your child do during this ferocious ostrich attack? Tell them to open the door leading out to their sandbox. If your punching attack fails, which it almost certainly will, lure the ostrich there. Then release a lion. The ostrich will immediately get spooked and bury its head in the sand, making it that much easier for the lion to eat it. It's a happy ending for everyone except the ostrich, which is fine because ostriches are the worst.

Don't have a lion in your backyard? That's an interesting life choice. I guess not everyone loves their family enough to keep them safe. Still, if you find yourself shamefully lion-deficient, you can spook the ostrich just by making lion noises. Seriously, I can't stress enough how dumb they are. But they are still taller than me, and I have to respect them for that. Maybe I'm part ostrich.

A SMALL BIRD IN THE HOUSE

An ostrich isn't the only bird that can break into your house, although it's by far the most likely. There's also a chance your home might be invaded by a regular bird, like a sparrow or a starling. This might not seem as bad as an ostrich attack, and it's not. It's much, much worse.

Songbirds are small, so they're harder to catch than ostriches. Plus they can fly. If ostriches could fly, that would be the end of human civilization. Or the start of a classic arcade game. Get ready to joust. Small birds use their altitude advantage to spread biocontaminants all over your house. They constantly poop and pee, which they do from the same hole at the same time, so even short bird incursions will bathe your house in unwanted bird juices. That could infect you with some deadly avian pathogen, like bird flu or chicken pox. Keep in mind, I'm not a doctor. Even if the bird spray doesn't make you sick, it will disgust you into retreat. Birds are experts at this kind of psychological warfare because they have no psychology to speak of. They're mindless Terminators with beaks.

Plus, science tells us birds of any size are dinosaurs. With big birds, you don't have time to think about it because they're physically attacking you, but with small birds, the creepiness factor has time to sink in. Just look at those scaly claws. Those are not the feet of an animal that wants to cuddle. Do you want a small dinosaur walking around your house? Worse, do you want one flying around it? That's what I thought.

The sooner the bird is out of your house, the better. But whatever you do, don't kill it. Dead birds are even grosser than live ones. Also, your kid will remember that you killed a bird and will tell everyone. Then other people will question why an adult was scared of such a small, harmless creature. And when you explain that birds are the devil and your pathological fear of them is fully justified, the state will have you committed. Just shoo out the bird and skip the drama. Unless the bird looks at you funny. Then get a flamethrower.

But assuming you're still on the nonlethal track, first open every door and window in your house. Next, grab a broom, tennis racket, or anything else you can swing. Don't actually swing it at the bird because you might hit it and then you'll have a fight on your hands. But kind of wave it in the bird's general direction. Just make sure you look unfriendly while you do it. The last thing you want is for the bird to think you're waving hello.

Unfortunately, herding birds is even harder than herding children. Your kid can only evade you on two planes, but a bird will dodge on three. The bird will refuse to exit through any of the openings due to a combination of confusion and actual malice. Keep the doors and windows open anyway as you chase the bird around your house. At least it will keep your house better ventilated as you try not to panic.

After several hours, you won't lose the bird, but your kid will lose all respect for you. Good. It was going to happen eventually. Might as well rip off that Band-Aid all at once.

If, by some miracle, the bird accidentally flies outside while you chase it, immediately close all the doors and windows. Then count how many other birds flew in the house while you were chasing the first one. Repeat this process as necessary until your house is bird-free or completely destroyed, whichever comes first.

PENGUINS

I know what you're thinking: Penguins would never kill my family. Famous last words. Although no one will know they were your last words if you only thought them. Unless you're facing telepathic penguins, in which case you're not reading this chapter anyway because you're already dead.

But assuming you're facing non-telepathic penguins—by far the most common variety—time is of the essence. By even being penguin-adjacent, your life and the life of your child are at risk. Most penguins live in the coldest, most inhospitable places on earth. They don't even need to attack. They can just stand there while you slowly freeze to death. Those jerks.

The first step to surviving is to make sure the penguins don't fatally distract you. They're so cute and fun to stare at that you might not realize your blood is slowly turning into the world's grossest slushie. This phenomenon is known as penguin blindness, and it means you only see penguins and not all the ways they can kill you and your child. To distract your kid from penguin blindness, hand them your phone. You won't miss it. At the South Pole, cell phone service is spotty at best. If you do have a few bars, though, save that phone for yourself. Always live-tweet your own death.

Unfortunately, safety isn't as simple as averting your eyes. If you're not looking at penguins, they can sneak attack. I don't know why they would, but I'm sure they have their reasons. It's not like you're the easiest person to get along with. Once the penguins launch an assault, you'll have no choice but to look at them. Go back to back with your kid as thousands of small tuxedo birds surround you, ready to peck you both to death. You'll only have one chance at survival, but it's a good one: Prepare to bowl.

Penguins are naturally slick. They shoot out of the water like torpedoes and slide across the ice. Use that against them. Grab a penguin near the front of the horde. Place one hand on its chest and use the other hand to firmly grasp its tail feathers. Pull back, then slide the penguin into the mass of advancing Antarctic birds. This should topple other penguins and possibly cause a domino effect through the entire flock. Grab the next penguin and slide it, too. Keep going until there are no penguins left standing. Your gloves should protect you from some of the penguin bites. Your bowling skills will protect you from the rest. But despite the bowling analogy, make sure you don't accidentally stick your fingers in any of the penguin's holes. That could really hurt the speed of your release.

Your kid should be able to bowl alongside you. Even the biggest penguin is only as tall as the average seven-year-old. Tell your kid to prioritize the smaller penguins while you focus on the bigger ones. It's a lifesaving battle strategy and a great bonding activity. Nothing cements a parent-child relationship like a good old-fashioned penguin war.

After you topple the flock, use your long, human legs to exit the icy field of battle before the penguins get back up. Retreat to someplace penguins don't live, and never leave. You don't need to return to Antarctica to finish off the penguins. Global warming will do that for you. Just keep living selfishly and humanity will triumph. Again.

How to Tell Different Penguin Species Apart

Type of Penguin	How to Identify It
Emperor Penguin	Has no clothes
King Penguin	Does the royal wave
Crested Penguin	Permanent bed head, despite never sleeping in a bed
Chinstrap Penguin	In a tiny biker gang
Southern Rockhopper Penguin	Drinks moonshine while hopping rocks
African Penguin	Confused about where penguins are supposed to live
Yellow-Eyed Penguin	Possessed by demons
Macaroni Penguin	Acts cheesy
Telepathic Penguin	Judges you for your weird daydream about the Smurfs

REINDEER

It's Christmas Eve. You're patiently waiting for a fat man in a red suit to climb down your chimney, but instead a reindeer crashes through your front window. Maybe Santa has been drinking. He has to do something to stay warm on those long winter nights. Or maybe the reindeer broke away from the sleigh to charge its own reflection in the glass. You just had to use Windex. Either way, now you have an angry, confused flying reindeer and a very upset child. What should you do?

First, assure your kid that Santa is okay. This may or may not be a lie. Santa's sleigh probably has enough redundancies to safely land while missing one reindeer. But in case it doesn't, don't go looking for Santa's body. Just stay inside and pray his corpse landed on somebody else's property. Fewer legal issues that way.

Next, deal with the reindeer. Reindeer have a few advantages over you in a fight. First, they have fuzzy antlers. That means they'll tickle when they stab you. Second, reindeer are strong. They pull an obese man and his infinite bag of toys. Tossing you aside won't be a problem. Third, magic reindeer can fly. They can smash up your ceiling as well as your walls and floors. And if they panic midair, they could belly-flop on you, which would be a pretty unique way to die. At least people would have something to talk about at your funeral.

Finally, flying reindeer are magical creatures. Most other magical creatures have one specific weakness but are invulnerable to almost everything else. Werewolves are vulnerable to silver bullets. Vampires are vulnerable to stakes. Anakin Skywalker is vulnerable to the high ground. But nobody knows the weakness of flying reindeer. People don't typically try to murder them. Whatever you do, don't post pictures of your kill on social media.

Your best bet is to avoid magical reindeer combat altogether. Open your front door. Then take the cookies meant for Santa and toss them outside. The reindeer should run out after them. Santa never shares, so the reindeer will have deep-seated sugar lust born from a lifetime of cookie deprivation. As soon as the reindeer sprints outside, lock the door. That's a job well done.

Of course, you still have a massive hole in your window, so the reindeer could fly back in to search for more cookies. That was poor planning on your part. When house hunting, you should have considered your home's defensive capabilities against reindeer. Also, you've now given that reindeer a dangerous cookie dependency. That's probably why Santa never shared his cookies with them in the first place. Why did you listen to me? I can't be held responsible for the things I write in my own book.

If the reindeer does reenter your house, you'll have to fight it, cookie addiction or no. Tell your kid to offer the reindeer whatever is in the fridge. The reindeer will be distracted by your gross leftovers, and that's when you'll attack. Push the Christmas tree over on top of the reindeer. With luck, the reindeer will get tangled in the strings of lights, immobilizing it. Without luck, you'll have a furious reindeer rampaging through your house with a Christmas tree stuck to its head. It could be worse, although I'm really not sure how. Maybe there could be two reindeer.

If the tree fails to take out the reindeer, shoo your child out of the way while you sedate the animal. It's doubtful that you have tranquilizer darts sitting around (if you did, you already would have used them on your kid), so try serving the reindeer a stiff drink. It's unlikely to trust you after you just tried to crush it beneath a Christmas tree, but remind the reindeer that it should forgive you in the spirit of the season. Then get it so drunk that it passes out and can be retrieved by the authorities or possibly Santa if he's not dead. Merry Christmas.

SHARKS

You're playing Marco Polo in the shallows with your kid when you hear dramatic cello music. That can only mean one thing: Your game is about to be crashed by a cartilage torpedo with teeth. I know, I know: Sharks are peaceful creatures who are more afraid of us than we are of them. But every year, at least a few people die in shark attacks. Maybe you and your kid found the elusive jerk shark. Or maybe a regular shark found a pair of not-so-elusive jerk humans. I'm not here to judge, just to help you survive, whether you deserve to or not.

As always, your top priority is to protect your kid. They're smaller and less likely to survive a shark attack. Also, they haven't had a chance to screw up their life yet. We already know how you turned out. If society can only keep one of you, let's gamble on the fresh start.

First, make sure the shark is actually attacking you. There's no reason to turn a passing shark into a dining shark. Clues that a shark is trying to eat you include: (1) It's circling you; (2) it's shooting up at you from the depths with its mouth wide open; (3) the tempo of the ominous background music increases dramatically; (4) one or more of your limbs is suddenly missing. If you're not in the water and you exhibit any of these symptoms, consult a licensed health professional. And keep an eye out for land sharks.

Once you're sure the shark is in attack mode, make yourself as appetizing a target as possible so the shark goes for you and not your kid. To do that, you'll need body mass. A shark wants a full meal, not a bite-sized snack. But it's hard to add mass on the spur of the moment. It takes years of bad decision making to get to that point. Chances are you've been doing that on your own anyway. As you get older, you don't get worse at physical activity; you get better at survival. Your body naturally clings to extra calories like your life depends on them because it might. If there were a sudden famine, husky middle-aged people would be more likely to survive than lean, fit twenty-somethings. And no one is better at adding extra weight than parents.

Those bonus pounds do more than make you a more tempting shark attack victim. They actually help you win the fight. Chances are you didn't add that extra mass by bingeing on health foods. You did it with preservatives, artificial dyes, and high-fructose corn syrup so concentrated it actually glowed. All those chemicals are permanently embedded in your fat cells. Your body is literally pulsating with toxins. One bite and that shark will go belly up. The most poisonous creature in the ocean isn't a blowfish; it's you.

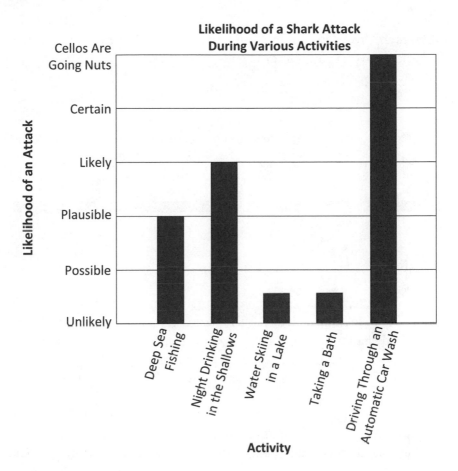

Likelihood of a Shark Attack During Various Activities

If that doesn't work, you have one last line of defense. Think about how gross it is to find a hair in your food. If that happened at a restaurant, you'd send back your meal. Sharks are used to eating smooth fish or mostly hair-less mammals like dolphins and whales. But you have a full head of hair. Pull off a few strands and stick them down the shark's throat. It will gag the shark up in no time.

But what if you're a healthy eater and also bald? You're going to die. At least your kid will make it safely to shore. Hopefully they'll learn from your mistakes and live a less healthy lifestyle while also maintaining a full head of hair. That's the best any of us can hope for our kids.

TIGERS

Tigers are the second-largest cat on earth. The first is the overfed domestic house cat. I'm looking at you, Garfield. But unlike their domesticated relative, nobody hands tigers trays of lasagna. Tigers have to actually earn their meals. And if you're not vigilant, that meal will be your kid.

Tiger-related fatalities in the US are currently hovering around zero, but only because the US doesn't have any tigers in the wild. If it did, the number of fatalities would be an amount greater than zero. That should keep you up at night, if only because math is unsettling, regardless of tiger attacks.

If anyone does encounter a tiger in the US, though, it will be you. The weirdest things always happen to parents, and besides, you probably found a quarter on the ground at some point, and now the universe has to even out that karma.

Tigers are big and powerful, but they're also cowards. This could be because humans have hunted them nearly to extinction, but it might also be because tigers naturally lack self-confidence. Whatever you do, don't give them a pep talk. A little self-esteem will get you killed.

Timid but deadly tigers prefer to strike from behind. Given children's natural lack of situational awareness, this makes kids especially vulnerable to attack. Children seldom look both ways before they cross the street and never look behind them in case of tiger attacks. Fortunately, as a parent, you have a natural defense against tigers: eyes in the back of your head. If any children are reading this book, that's not a metaphor. Parents can literally see behind them at all times, so it's pointless to get away with anything. It's just one of our 725 distinct superpowers.

To keep your kid safe from tigers, you'll have to use these backward-facing eyes to protect them. Keep your child nearby at all times, no matter how much you think more quality time might kill you. Time apart will kill your kid, if a tiger is around. If you see a tiger sneaking up behind your kid, yell, "Hey, that's a tiger!" Being self-conscious, the tiger will slink away to cheer for a mediocre baseball team or endorse an okay breakfast cereal. Since your child won't have seen the tiger, you can also claim there were tigers even if there weren't any. If you remind your child constantly that you drive away unseen predators, your kid will love you more. And if they don't, let them get eaten by tigers. You can always have more kids.

WOOLLY MAMMOTHS

You're out playing with your child in the snow when a woolly mammoth tries to trample you both. That's disappointing because woolly mammoths are supposed to be extinct. You have a valid complaint against your cave-man ancestors. Their one job was to kill everything that moved, and they let us all down. Find the nearest time-traveling mail carrier and send an angry letter. Make liberal use of exclamation points.

The fastest way to escape the mammoth is to dive on top of your child's sled and slide down the hill with them. Just be sure you don't accidentally flatten your kid before the woolly mammoth has a chance to flatten you both. Your swift escape should make the woolly mammoth lose interest. Seriously, they're not that smart. Otherwise they wouldn't have let cavemen hunt them to extinction. Or extinction save for one.

If the woolly mammoth pursues you down the hill, roll to the side with your child and let the beast run past. That's a lot of mass going down a slick hill. Perhaps the mammoth will keep going and run off a cliff. I don't know why you would take your kid sledding near a cliff, but I'm here to save your child from mammoths, not from you.

If you're not near a cliff and the woolly mammoth turns at the bottom of the hill to come back for you, consider your options carefully. Are you strong enough to defeat a woolly mammoth in hand-to-hand combat? Even if you are, that won't save you since this would be hand-to-trunk combat, a fighting scenario addressed by neither karate nor jiujitsu. If you were looking for a niche to break into the martial-arts training market, there it is.

Since you can't outfight a mammoth, you'll have to out-think it. Open a dialogue with the mammoth. Stress how the mammoth is all by itself. No matter how many people it kills, it will still die alone. Hopefully the mammoth will become depressed enough to die on the spot. If not, the mammoth will almost certainly smash you, but at least by then your kid will be back inside your house, probably drinking hot chocolate. They would have prepared a mug for you, but your survival was always unlikely, and besides, sharing is the worst. Even if you're only a very flat memory to your kid, your child will grow up forever remembering that they should drive every large land animal to extinction, even the peaceful herbivores. Lesson learned.

Warning: If the animal you're facing is a mastodon and not a woolly mammoth, none of these steps will work. Remember, a woolly mammoth is a hairy brown elephant, but a mastodon is a hairy brown elephant. See the difference? If not, consult this handy chart.

The Differences Between Woolly Mammoths and Mastodons

Attribute	Woolly Mammoth	Mastodon
Color	Brown	Brownish brown
Diet	Only plants	Not meat
Legs	More than three but less than five	Less than five but more than three
Favorite Yoga Pose	Downward dog	Child's pose
Favorite Tom Hanks Movie	*Forrest Gump*	*Apollo 13*
Sex in the City character	Miranda	Charlotte
Reason for Extinction	Hunted by humans	Ate Pop Rocks and soda
Descendant	Modern elephants	Mr. Snuffleupagus

BEAST MASTER

Animals pose an existential threat to you and your child. After reading through this chapter, you might wish animals didn't exist at all. I get it. But no matter how much we want to, we can't simply eliminate all the creatures of the earth. Animals serve vital roles, like starring in viral videos and being food. That's about it, but it's enough. A life without steak and cats startled by cucumbers is no life at all.

As you protect your child from all of nature's terrible creations, keep these dos and don'ts in mind:

✓ **Do** be suspicious of all animals. The cuter, the more deadly. This rule also applies to children.

✗ **Don't** trust your pets. Remember, cats and dogs are apex predators. They won't hesitate to eat you if you die, or just take a really intense nap.

✓ **Do** watch for signs that animals are nearby. Those scratch marks on a tree could be a sign of a bobcat, a tiger, or a squirrel with metal Wolverine claws. Guard your nuts.

✗ **Don't** take your child to the zoo. It will give your kid the false impression that the goats in the petting zone are domestic friends, not lurking murder beasts.

✓ **Do** respect all animals. You never know what small, harmless creature might step in ooze and become a teenage mutant ninja.

✗ **Don't** feed wild animals. A pigeon's brain is too small to tell the difference between bread crumbs and your delicious face.

✓ **Do** learn about animals. It's critical to know your enemies. That's why you know so much about yourself.

✗ **Don't** trust the experts. When a lepidopterist tells you a butterfly can't kill you, it's only because they're taking bribes to spread pro-butterfly propaganda.

With that, you're officially ready to protect your child against all the animals of the earth. Or at least against the specific ones I mentioned in this chapter. For the rest, you'll have to wing it. Or buy the sequel.

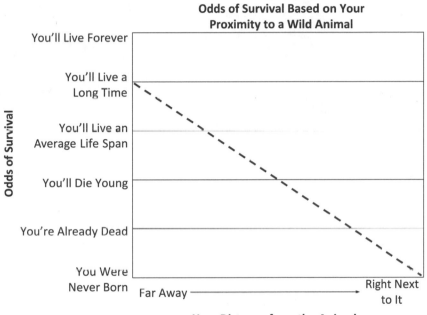

CHAPTER 3

SUPERNATURAL BEINGS

Some things defy the laws of physical reality. Chief among them are ghosts, monsters, and your own children. All are the stuff of nightmares. To keep your little monsters safe from the other monsters of the world, you'll need to use all your parenting skills. If you don't have any, just use this book. Not directly, though. Swinging a small paperback is seldom effective against incorporeal beings. But give it a try anyway. At the very least, you'll produce a light breeze. Fighting monsters is hot work.

Just because something doesn't show up on a scientific instrument doesn't mean it isn't a threat. If supernatural beings don't exist, then why are humans universally afraid of them? Our subconscious mind can sense danger our conscious mind cannot. Either that or our primitive monkey brains are helplessly paranoid about anything that goes bump in the night. I choose to believe we're terrified for a reason, mainly because I'm so good at being afraid. We have nothing to fear but literally everything.

GHOSTS

You move your family into a house only to discover there's a ghost. It wants you out—now. What should you do?

Run? Hide? Burn down the house and start a new life funded by insurance fraud?

No.

You're basically at war with a whiny bedsheet.

Bring it on.

Ghosts don't kill people. If they did, they would be unstoppable ethereal assassins who could take over the world. But have you ever seen a ghost take out world leaders and bend entire nations to their will? No. They mostly just make annoying noises in the dark and sometimes push a door open. If those are the best powers you get from being a disembodied soul, I'll stick with being alive, thank you very much.

Most of the time, a ghost's entire goal is to make you leave a house. I can sympathize. Guests are the worst. But once you buy a place, retreating because of a ghost isn't an option. The only thing more eternal than a soul is a mortgage.

Why do ghosts want you to leave? Apparently they're extreme introverts who can't deal with even minor disruptions to their solitude. You have a kid. Checkmate.

There's nothing scarier to a ghost than a child. A kid doesn't care if you're a floating, semitransparent being from another plane of existence.

A child has no idea how the world is supposed to work. Kids make up ten imaginary friends an hour who are just as messed up as a ghost and—to your child—just as real. You can't out-weird a kid. Don't even try.

That's why ghosts don't even attempt to scare kids. All ghostly theatrics—creepy sounds, floating objects, tidal waves of blood surging through the hallways—are aimed squarely at adults. To a kid, that stuff is child's play. There's never a point in a normal childhood when a kid isn't making irritating noises. They make stuff fly across the room all the time, usually by throwing it. The more fragile an object, the more likely it is to go airborne. And as for the tidal waves of blood, your child won't even notice it over all the other stains they've made. After a few Kool-Aid spills, every house looks like a murder scene.

More than anything, ghosts are scared of your child tearing down the house. Let them. If it comes down to it, you can get a new house. The ghost can't. It's a battle of wills, and the house is your hostage. The ghost loves the house so much that it plans to spend eternity there. And your child could burn the whole thing to the ground in a single unsupervised afternoon. The ghost is right to be afraid. It might be an unholy spirit, but it didn't encounter true evil until it met your kid.

Even if your child doesn't destroy the house, a ghost is still no match for them. Spirits want isolation and quiet, and that's the opposite of living with a child. Rattling chains in the attic can't compete with a 24/7 temper tantrum. The only thing louder than a kid when they're mad is a kid when they're happy. The ghost will be powerless to do anything but wish it were even deader as your child sings the same song ten thousand times in a row. I'm sure the ghost will enjoy having that song stuck in its head for the rest of its afterlife. Eternity just got a whole lot longer.

The worst part for the ghost is that it's trapped. It wants you to move out because it can't. For whatever reason, it has to stay at this address forever. It can't even kill itself to escape. Double death isn't a thing. Not even for Scientologists.

That's why ghosts talk to kids rather than trying to scare them. When your child says they had a conversation with a mysterious figure who looks just like the home's old caretaker who died a hundred years ago tonight, the ghost isn't being creepy. It's trying to negotiate. It's hoping that maybe—just maybe—if it befriends your child, it can keep your kid quiet long enough for it to scare you into moving out. Do the opposite and settle in for life.

Best-case scenario, the ghost keeps your child entertained and becomes a de facto babysitter. It has to protect your child. If your kid dies, they'll become a ghost, too, and the original ghost will be stuck with your kid for even longer. Worst-case scenario, your kid goes back to making noise and browbeats the ghost into submission. Either way, you win. All your parent friends will wish their kids had free nontemporal babysitters, too.

But what if your kid is away at Grandma's house for the weekend? Never fear. You have a device that can keep ghosts at bay, no exorcism required. There's never been a clear, convincing photo of a ghost. If all else fails, keep your phone in front of you with the camera app pulled up. Any ghost in your way will have no choice but to dematerialize lest you prove its existence. And if it doesn't hide, you'll have an awesome picture you can sell to the highest bidder. Congrats on your newfound career as a ghost hunter. Enjoy your reality show.

Not only should you not avoid ghosts, you should actively seek out the homes where they reside. You'll get a discount on the purchase price plus free ghost day care. Nobody else wants to move into an infamous house where a family just like yours was tragically murdered. Their loss.

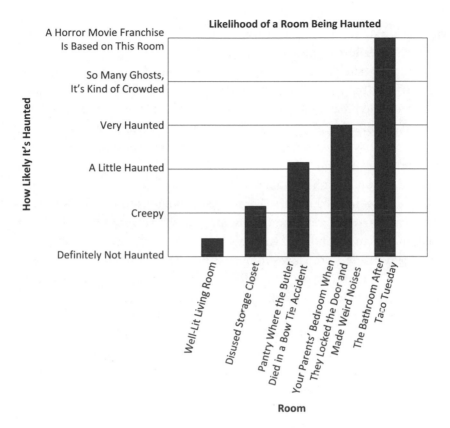

Likelihood of a Room Being Haunted

How Likely It's Haunted (y-axis):
- A Horror Movie Franchise Is Based on This Room
- So Many Ghosts, It's Kind of Crowded
- Very Haunted
- A Little Haunted
- Creepy
- Definitely Not Haunted

Room (x-axis):
- Well-Lit Living Room
- Disused Storage Closet
- Pantry Where the Butler Died in a Bow Tie Accident
- Your Parents' Bedroom When They Locked the Door and Made Weird Noises
- The Bathroom After Taco Tuesday

VAMPIRES

Contrary to popular belief, vampires are dangerous, not romantic. There's nothing sexy about a well-dressed corpse. Edward might be the hottest cadaver, but he's still just another dead body. The competition is stiff.

Vampires are especially deadly around children. A vampire can't enter your home unless it's invited. If your child opens the door for a vampire—probably after you specifically tell them not to—there's a 100 percent chance your child will invite that vampire inside. Prepare your defenses with the idea that the vampire will already be in your house. When children are involved, failure is the starting point.

Vampires hate garlic, but not because it harms them in any way. They just don't like the smell. They might drink blood, but they still get squeamish about bad breath. I recommend feeding your kid foods heavy in garlic. Your child won't like them, just like they don't like anything else with actual flavor. Their loss. Eat their garlic-saturated leftovers yourself to repel vampires and other human beings. When it comes to defending your personal space, all options are on the table.

A vampire dies when you drive a stake through its heart. That's not particularly surprising. Pretty much anything dies if you stab it in the heart, except maybe an artichoke. If you walk into your house and discover a vampire already inside—probably sitting on the couch as your child regales them with round ninety-nine of "watch this"—don't be surprised. Most vampires will pass on your child to wait for you. If vampires are squeamish about garlic breath, they'll definitely be repulsed by your kid, who is far grosser in so many ways. Let's be honest: A few bath nights a week aren't enough. If you want to keep your child clean, you need to hose them down twice daily.

With the vampire still distracted, stab it from behind. Yes, you can get to the heart from the front or the back, as long as you have a basic understanding of anatomy. The heart is the big organ in the middle of the chest that goes "thump thump." Just don't expect your child to congratulate you on your kill. The vampire was actually paying attention to them. You killed their new best friend, you monster.

Vampires won't always come to you in human form. They can also appear as bats. You probably have some in your attic right now. Are they vampire bats? Absolutely. That's just how old houses work. To get rid of vampire bats in your attic, don't have an attic. If that isn't an option, go up there and hang crucifixes everywhere. Crosses don't hurt vampires. Vampires just leave because they get tired of you pushing your religion on them. You are to them what Jehovah's Witnesses are to everybody else. Knock knock.

What about if your child is bitten by a vampire? Depending on which lore is right, your child might become a vampire themselves. Can you live with a vampire? If you have a teenager, you basically already do. They stay up all night, and first thing in the morning they're dead to the world. Just because your kid occasionally goes outside during the day doesn't mean they're not undead. There's no evidence that sunlight actually hurts vampires. Really, there's no evidence for anything about vampires. The occult sciences are tragically underfunded.

But ethically, is it okay to raise a vampire child? Vampires don't age. If your child is a vampire, they'll be a child for life. Then again, in the era of extended adolescence, they were never going to mature anyway, so what difference does it make?

At least your vampire child will be easier to feed than a regular human kid. They'll want blood and only blood, which doesn't require any cooking. Where they get that blood will be up to you. You could try the butcher shop, or you could let your child hunt for themselves. Tell them to only suck the blood of animals and don't ask any follow-up questions. Your top priority is to protect yourself from liability, not to protect other people from your kid. That's what parenting is all about.

Personally, I think it's a good idea to stop your child from becoming a vampire, but only because the vampire transition is permanent. You wouldn't let your nine-year-old get a tattoo, so you shouldn't let them become an eternal minion of the damned. Grade school is too early to pick a career for life—and after.

Common Misconceptions About Vampires

Misconception	Reality
They're refined and cultured.	They slurp when they drink.
They prefer to stay in high school.	They'd rather go anywhere else, including hell.
They naturally sparkle.	Glitter follows you everywhere, even the grave.
They form elaborate vampire societies.	Making friends is even harder after you die.
They want to seduce a human mate.	Even eternity isn't long enough for that kind of drama.
They're obsessed with goth outfits.	They mostly wear yellow reflective vests for safer night travel.
They have to sleep in coffins.	They choose to sleep in coffins. It beats dealing with skeezy mattress stores.
They wear capes.	They wear sweater vests. Much better for heating the core.
They're awesome.	They suck.

MUMMIES

Mummy attacks are rare in North America, mostly due to a severe shortage of Egyptian pyramids outside Egypt. Few American politicians are brave enough to address this unequal pyramid distribution, so dead pharaoh shortfalls continue unabated. If your dream is to die of an ancient Egyptian curse but you live in the US, you're probably out of luck.

Unless, of course, there's a traveling museum exhibit. It's likely the only place outside of Egypt that your child will ever see a mummy. Few parents take their children to cursed burial chamber excavations anymore. And that's why we're falling behind China.

If you and your child are attacked by a mummy at the museum, here's what to do.

First, inform the mummy that neither you nor your child disturbed its tomb. You merely paid a small fee to gawk at its dried-out corpse after somebody else did the tomb raiding for you. That's totally different.

If the mummy seems unpersuaded—which is likely, given the language barrier—prepare for battle. Keep the mummy distracted with more excuses about how nothing is ever your fault. Meanwhile, have your child sneak around behind the mummy. If your kid is under the age of five, they'll feel an irresistible urge to unravel the once mighty king like a giant roll of toilet paper. The mummy will be stripped naked, causing it to die of exposure or embarrassment. Egyptian curses are no match for human shame.

If your child is older, however, when they sneak around behind the mummy, they might just keep going and walk out of the museum. Maybe they'll get help. But more likely, they'll forget all about you because they're texting a friend. Either way, be prepared to solve the situation on your own.

Mummies are vulnerable to fire. So is everything else—except maybe sharks. Even then, an underwater welding torch would probably do the trick. If you happen to have napalm with you when confronting a mummy, this would be a good time to use it. If not, a cigarette lighter will do. I'm not encouraging you to smoke. Cigarettes will kill you long before a mummy ever will. But if you have that terrible habit anyway, you might as well benefit from the one and only upside of nicotine addiction, which is increased preparedness for a mummy attack.

If fire isn't an option, you'll have to lead the mummy on a chase through the museum. The mummy won't be very spry. Being cooped up in a sarcophagus for a few thousand years will do that to you. Of course, you aren't very spry, either. You and the pharaoh probably last went to the gym around the same time. Do your best to run anyway.

Weave around fragile museum exhibits. Mummies are clumsy, so they'll bump into artifacts and break them. You're clumsy, too, so you'll do the same. Blame all the destruction on the mummy. The mummy will be too busy dealing with the bill for escalating damages to keep chasing you. Those docents don't mess around.

If the museum curator tries to stick you with the bill as well, remind them that their exhibit tried to kill you. The museum will let you off the hook so you don't sue them. Either that or they'll murder you and throw you in the pharaoh's sarcophagus as part of an elaborate cover-up. Only attend non-evil museums just in case.

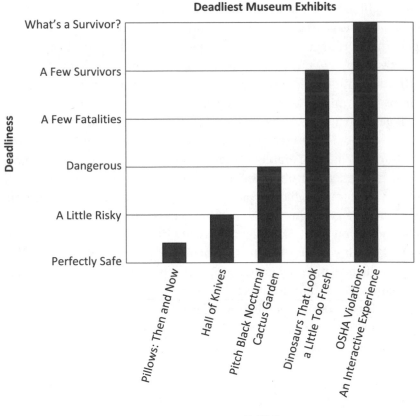

Deadliest Museum Exhibits

WEREWOLVES

Werewolves only appear during a full moon, but that doesn't lessen the threat they pose to you and your child. Never doubt the power of something that comes once a month to complicate your life. Most of the time, werewolves are just regular people who might not even know they're a werewolf. But even if they do know, you can't ask them. That information is protected by HIPAA.

The only thing that can kill a werewolf is a silver bullet. Chances are you don't carry those in your diaper bag. I'd recommend you start, but you probably carry fifty or sixty pounds of gear with you already. To take a gun and silver bullets with you to the park, you'll have to leave something else heavy at home. I recommend your child.

Fortunately, as with almost any other problem in life, there are ways to deal with a werewolf besides shooting it. A werewolf is part wolf, and a wolf is just a dog. That means that werewolves have the same behavioral flaws as man's best friend. Instead of silver bullets, carry a tennis ball. When a werewolf attacks, throw the ball one direction and take off in the opposite one. Just make sure you drag your kid with you so they don't chase the ball, too.

What if the werewolf doesn't chase the ball? Smack it in the nose with a newspaper. Don't subscribe to the newspaper? Of course you don't. The last print newspaper went extinct in 1984. But you do have electronic devices that can display news articles. Pick up your phone or tablet and smack the werewolf in the nose with it. The tempered glass won't break, but the were-wolf's face might.

After you establish dominance, the werewolf will submit by rolling over so you can rub its belly. Don't. That's a good way to lose your hand or your dignity. If the werewolf turns back into a person while you're petting it, you'll never be able to look each other in the eye again. It's happened to me twice.

MONSTERS UNDER THE BED

Whether or not there's a monster under your kid's bed is a topic of intense debate among literally no one because every parent is pretty sure monsters don't exist. The scariest thing around your kid's bed is your kid.

But for the sake of discussion, let's say there really is a monster under your kid's bed. It's a threat worth taking seriously. You'll look like a terrible parent if you check on your child in the morning and discover they were eaten overnight. As a parent, it's your job to obsess over all dangers, both real and imagined. The threats that don't exist are the most dangerous ones of all. Just ask anyone on the internet, who will be happy to point out all the imaginary things you should be afraid of.

The easiest way to eliminate the threat of a monster under your kid's bed is to make sure there is no "under the bed." Set your child's mattress directly on the ground. Your kid is too young for lower back problems, so there won't be any negative effects, aside from the slight risk of smashing the monster under the bed. If it smells like something died under there, grab an air freshener. As a bonus, putting your child's bed on the floor will prepare them for early adulthood. Right out of college, they won't be able to afford a bed frame. It's the sleeping arrangement of choice for the young, independent, and slightly pathetic. What a great preview of the worst period of their life.

If you insist on keeping your child's mattress elevated, you could surround the bottom of your kid's bed with chicken wire. Although if the monster made it all the way into your child's bedroom without being detected, there's a good chance it doesn't obey Newtonian physics. The fourth law of motion is any body part outside the covers gets eaten after dark.

In that case, prepare your child to deal with the monster when it finally shows itself. Since your kid is unlikely to prevail in unarmed combat, have your child tell the monster about that new cartoon your kid loves but you don't understand at all. Your child's uninterrupted fifty-minute monologue will give you enough time to leisurely stroll in and intervene. Or to close your bedroom door and put a pillow over your head. If the monster is willing to sit through that lecture, it deserves a free meal.

MONSTERS IN THE CLOSET

You might think a monster in the closet is the same as a monster under the bed, but you couldn't be more wrong. For one thing, a monster under the bed is under the bed, while a monster in the closet is in the closet. Those are two completely different places. Another difference is closet monsters can be much larger than under-the-bed monsters because closet monsters have more space.

The obvious exception is if your child sleeps in a loft bed, in which case why are you such a terrible parent? But usually closet monsters are bigger. If you have a walk-in closet, your child's monster could be the size of an SUV. HGTV downplays those dream-house dangers. They're part of the cover-up.

So how can you protect your child from a closet monster? For starters, put a lock on the outside of the closet door. Just don't let your kid get locked in or child protective services will get involved. I'd rather deal with the closet monster.

If locks are out of the question, repel monsters by living like you normally do. Keep all closets chaotic and disorganized. This should be easy with a child in the house. Let the storage space naturally fall into disarray until anyone or anything that opens it will be crushed by falling debris. No monster will go in the closet after that. Monster OSHA won't let them.

If there's already a monster in the closet and it's too late to clutter them out, board up the closet and plaster or drywall it to make it look like part of the wall. Secret closets are charming and not creepy at all. That's a lie. But it probably won't be an issue unless you try to sell the house. Just remember to unhide the closets before the open house and to declare any known monsters on the disclosure forms.

Alternatively, if you're reasonably confident the monster is imaginary, you could tell your child you've already made the monster closet disappear and that the only remaining closet in the room is the one that's monster-free. That will make your kid less afraid of closets but more afraid of random spots on the wall. In the parenting world, that's called progress.

The end result of the secret-closet plan may be that your child becomes terrified of their room. Depending on their age, this could be a good thing. Maybe they'll venture out into the rest of the house so you'll actually see them sometimes. This will only work until their teenage years, when their aversion to hanging out with you will surpass their aversion to death. Then they'll take their chances with the hidden wall monster.

There is a downside to this brilliant idea. If your child is young, they'll flee their room and try to sleep in your bed. Explain to your kid that your room has even more secret closets full of monsters than theirs does. Your child might never sleep again, but at least they'll endure that insomnia in their own room, which of course has the fewest secret closets in the house. Just don't let them see a blueprint of the place or your house of cards will come crashing down. Note: A house of cards also has secret closets.

DRAGONS

Nobody knows why dragons hoard treasure. They never spend or invest it. There's no such thing as a dragon Roth IRA. Dragons simply sit on the money. It can't be that comfortable, either. They should use some of that gold to buy a couch.

Since the coins serve no utilitarian purpose, we can only assume dragons hoard them simply because gold is shiny. Dragons are basically giant, fire-breathing raccoons. At least you're smart enough to leave them alone. Too bad your child isn't.

Kids love finding coins. At the grocery store, they're not afraid to get down on their hands and knees in search of a gross penny stuck to the floor. Children also don't respect boundaries. They'll crawl under somebody's legs to pick up what they regard as free money. In a store, that's mildly embarrassing. In a dragon's lair, it's fatal.

If your child sneaks off to steal gold coins from a dragon, you'll have to act fast. Determine if your kid has the one ring to rule them all (see chapter nine). If they do, they can turn invisible and escape danger. Hopefully your child will stay quiet as they skulk around, but it's more likely they'll hum an annoying, nameless tune since that's just what children do. If you hear them making noise, shout into the lair that they need to be quiet. Your kid will reply, "I AM BEING QUIET." On second thought, don't say anything. Just sneak into the lair yourself.

If the dragon senses your child, distract it by throwing coins. The dragon will quickly zero in on you, so be prepared to negotiate. Tell the dragon that you'll reveal the location of an even bigger treasure hoard if the dragon spares your life. Then send the dragon on an epic, meandering quest, at the end of which the dragon will discover the treasure wasn't gold—of which there is none—but the friendships they made along the way. Then the dragon will incinerate you. But that should buy your kid the one thing money can't: enough time to escape.

If your child does get away with treasure, the dragon will retaliate by destroying the nearest human settlement. Let it. This isn't your fight. You're a parent, not a hero—unless you took my earlier advice, in which case you're just a pile of ashes on the floor.

The Dangers Posed by Different Types of Dragons

Type	Danger
Green	Cares about the environment. After killing you, will compost your body.
Red	Anger issues, but finds healthy outlets. Killing you is more therapeutic than Prozac.
Blue	Depressed, but killing you will cheer it up.
Yellow	Afraid of not killing you fast enough.
Violet	Sounds like violence. Or violins. Either musical or deadly.
Indigo	I don't know what color this is.
Black	Never gets a fair shake from the dragon police.
White	Breath weapon is pumpkin spice.

LEPRECHAUNS

A leprechaun's pot of gold is a threat to everyone, including your child. Where did it come from? If leprechauns magically created it, that means they can make precious metals out of nothing. Hello, hyperinflation. No prize at the end of the rainbow is worth destroying the economy.

Worse, if the leprechauns didn't magically create the gold, then they must have dug it up themselves in their secret leprechaun mines. That's adorable and possibly cruel. I can't imagine leprechauns pay a fair wage to their forced laborers. Also, where's the environmental impact study? Secret mines seldom report hazardous spills in a timely fashion. We could all be drinking toxic leprechaun runoff and not even know it. Secret leprechaun mines literally make me sick.

In popular culture, the negative economic and environmental impacts of leprechauns are glossed over because of the glitz and glamour of their three wishes. But the wishes are yet another chance to ruin human society. If you think a magical pot of gold is bad, wait until someone wishes for infinite money. And in the hands of your kid, that's exactly what will happen—if you're lucky.

If you're unlucky, your kid will wish for something minor that still blows up in their face. If they wish to be famous, they'll be all over the news for being kidnapped. If they wish to land on the moon, they'll get sent there without a spacesuit. If they wish for a horse, they'll just get Jell-O and glue. Always specify that you want your livestock alive and intact. That's Wishing 101.

Train your kid to run away from any leprechaun they see. Of course, your kid will ignore you and try to capture them instead. If your child can snag snakes and frogs, they can catch a tiny humanoid with magical powers. How else would we know about them? If leprechauns were effective at using their magic, they would rule the earth. Instead, they sneak around in unfashionable green suits, appearing in the open only occasionally to shill breakfast cereal. Maybe that's how they get their gold.

If your child actually manages to capture a leprechaun, tell them to turn it over to you. You, in turn, should turn it over to me. You'll know I got my hands on a leprechaun if this book ends up on the *New York Times* best-seller list. Or if this book exists at all. Seriously, without a magic spell, what kind of a publisher would print a guide that treats leprechauns as a serious threat to your child? A wise one, that's who.

Wishes That Always Backfire

Wish	How It Backfires
Immortality	You'll be an old person forever.
Resurrect the Dead	You're giving somebody all of their problems back.
Mind Reading	And you thought your mind was sick.
Wealth	Taxes.
Happiness	You'll be the jerk smiling at a funeral.

Love	Someone will love you unconditionally, and you'll immediately be sick of them.
World Peace	All humans will disappear.
Children	Children.

LIVING FURNITURE

You're sitting at home with your family minding your own business when suddenly your furniture attacks. It's just like that fortune cookie warned you. When a dessert predicts your exact cause of death, you better believe it. Or maybe just eat at a different restaurant.

When furniture comes to life, it will want to fight. There's no other reason for it to be alive. It's not like it spontaneously became sentient to tell you how much it loves the smell of your butt. The furniture will resent your family for years of abuse and stains. In fact, it was probably those stains that combined and mutated to give the furniture life. This is something that could really happen based on leading germ research I just made up. You don't have to understand it; you just have to survive it. That's how science works.

The more dinged up the furniture is, the more motivated it is to kill you. Even inanimate objects can only take so much abuse, and around children, that's all they'll get. The average life span of furniture in a family with kids is thirty-five seconds. Stain-guarding products are a sham. No chemical can match your child's supernatural ability to ruin all they touch.

Given those criteria, your couch is the most likely candidate to start the fight. Its surface supports more life-forms than a coral reef. The list of other furniture certain to come to life includes cribs, computer chairs, rugs, and anything that's been in or near your child's playroom. If your child doesn't have a designated playroom, the entire house is their playroom, and that means everything is coming for you. A fully furnished house is a deadly house. Remember that the next time you redecorate.

For this scenario, let's assume your child spills one glob of French onion dip too many, and it sends your couch over the line from gross and unsanitary to sentient and malevolent. How will it attack? If the furniture fight scene in Disney's animated *Beauty and the Beast* is scientifically accurate—and I can only assume it is—the couch's arms will function as arms, its legs will work as legs, and its cushions will form a mouth. It won't have teeth, but it won't need them. It will simply pull your kid inside the cushions, where it will dissolve your child using years of built-up corrosive odors. Expect the couch's arms to be quite efficient at punching, even if they're padded. That soft material will be worn down to nothing thanks to years of overuse, so the couch will basically be punching you with pieces of wood covered by a thin layer of fabric. Imagine that you've spent the last ten years sitting on a hibernating grizzly bear, and that bear suddenly wakes up. That's the kind of fight you're in for. Prepare accordingly.

When the couch attacks, your first step should be to check if it's still under warranty. The last thing you want is to blow a chance to get your money back. Perhaps the manufacturer would be willing to send you a replacement couch that's somewhat less murderous. Most likely, though, you're out of luck. By now, you've committed countless acts on that couch that violate the warranty, common decency, and the law. Now might be a good time to reexamine your life choices. Just kidding. Introspection is for the childless. On to the fight.

If you can, lure the couch out of the house. The couch might still murder several members of your family, but at least it won't make a mess on the floor. Bloodbaths are an outside sport. If it's raining, the water will solve all your problems. Everybody knows couches can't handle water. A soggy couch isn't an angry couch, just a sad and mopey one. If it isn't raining, grab a hose or a bucket of water and try to soak it that way instead. Your attack should be devastating. There's a reason couches don't enter wet T-shirt contests.

If there's no water available when you get outside, stand in the pocket and start trading blows. You can't out-punch a couch. Even a small love seat is Mike Tyson compared to you. There's a reason they don't let sentient couches participate in Olympic boxing. But you're not trying to win, you're just trying to buy some time. As you stand there, slugging it out, invite your child to sit on the couch. This might be challenging since the couch will be swinging its arms wildly in an attempt to kill you, but tell your child to do their best. Let them take whatever food, art supplies, and yard tools they want. This is their chance to use the couch in all the ways they've always

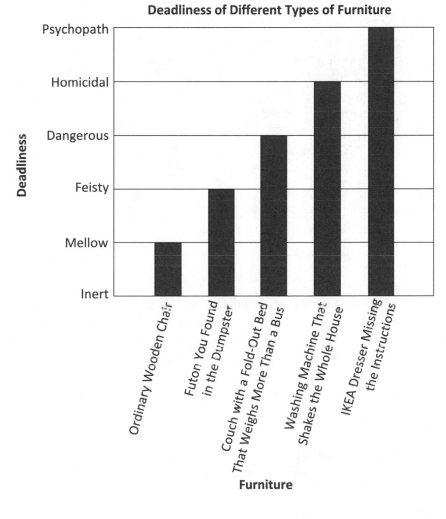

Deadliness of Different Types of Furniture

dreamed. If the couch is distracted enough to let your kid get close, your child should naturally destroy it just by being themselves. Within seconds, the couch will be a shredded pile of wood, stuffing, and fabric. Then have your kid call 911 because you'll undoubtedly have a couch-induced concussion. Make sure the paramedics know a fighting couch hit you in the head, not that getting hit in the head made you think you fought a couch. The order matters.

Once you make it to the hospital, everyone should be safe—as long as your kid doesn't sit on any of the waiting room furniture. The last thing you want is to set off round two.

UNSPOOKED

If you follow the suggestions I laid out here, you should be able to protect yourself and your child against practically any supernatural adversary, including ones I didn't discuss in this section. If you've seen one monster, you've seen them all. Just don't tell them I said that. Saying all supernatural creatures look the same is kind of racist.

As you protect your child against the interchangeable minions of hell, keep these dos and don'ts in mind:

✓ **Do** treat the undead with the respect they deserve, which is none. They're here to kill you and your kid, whether you're nice to them or not.

- ✘ **Don't** get too tied up with theology. Nobody cares which religion was right about the afterlife. Just try not to get sent there to find out.

- ✓ **Do** assume any structure you're in is maliciously haunted. You can't afford to let down your guard in that Porta-Potty.

- ✘ **Don't** waste time saying that you don't believe in the supernatural. The werewolf biting your leg won't care if you believe in it or not.

- ✓ **Do** pack snacks. There's no sense in fending off evil on an empty stomach.

- ✘ **Don't** split up. Dividing into groups is responsible for 100 percent of all horror movie fatalities.

- ✓ **Do** suppress your natural curiosity. You shouldn't care where ghosts come from. You should just care that you don't become one of them.

- ✘ **Don't** feel guilty if you and your kid are the only ones to survive. Every good horror story needs someone to live to tell the tale. Every good horror story also needs cannon fodder.

With that, you're ready to take on all the forces of the spirit world. Just not all at once. Hopefully they come at you one at a time, like in a bad kung fu movie. If they bunch up and attack in a group, you're screwed.

CHAPTER 4

PEOPLE

So far, we've covered a wide variety of ferocious creatures, both living and dead. The greatest threat to your child, other than your child, isn't a roving tiger or an astral being from beyond the physical realm. It's other people. We're as good at harming each other as we are at harming our world. No other force in heaven or on earth can match our destructive power. It feels good to be the best.

The only thing that can beat a human is another human. Luckily, that's what you are. Probably. If not, I apologize for assuming your species. Even as a human, it will take all of your wits to outsmart individuals who are out to harm you and your child. Why would they want to harm you? Many reasons. Perhaps they're evil. Or jealous. Or bored. Having nothing better to do has led to some of the worst disasters in human history. If the Kaiser had joined a bowling league, we could have avoided World War I.

While I can't prepare you against every way other human beings might threaten your child, I can guide you through a few of the most likely scenarios. Assume everyone else is just like you. We live in a world of monsters.

BLACK FRIDAY SALES

If you add up all the casualties from the battles of Gettysburg, Verdun, and the Bulge, you would have almost as much carnage as a typical Black Friday sale. But the lives lost in pursuit of savings don't accomplish anything of historic importance. In fact, those sacrifices are the opposite of heroism. Rather than fighting for a cause, people are fighting for material gain for themselves and their kids. Not that there's anything wrong with that. Bring on the discounts.

As dangerous as Black Friday sales are, it's still plausible you might take your kid to one. Maybe there was nobody else to watch your child at 4 AM, or perhaps there were plenty of people but no one wanted to enable your selfish life decisions. That's fine. Every person who betrayed you is just one less person to shop for.

If you have your child with you at a Black Friday sale, you have an advantage over other shoppers waiting in line outside the store. Your kid can hold your place in line while you leave to get more firewood to stave off hypothermia. I hope that half-price TV is worth it. (Spoiler alert: It is.) Just make sure to dress your child warmly enough. If they lose their fingers to frostbite, they won't be able to work the remote control. Although that would put you permanently in charge of what to watch. Just try not to seem too happy about it.

Inside the store, put your kid in a shopping cart, even if they're a teenager. The bigger they are, the more leverage they'll give you when you plow through the crowd. Never use your elbows when a battering ram will do. For added clearing power, have your kid stick out their arms to clothesline other shoppers. If anyone tries to retaliate, your child can duck down inside the shopping cart and be safe from most directions of attack. Shopping carts are the perfect offensive and defensive vehicle. It's a wonder nobody uses them in war.

But breaking through to the item you want is only half the battle. You also have to get out of the store with it. Make sure your child stays in the cart, no matter how big the item is. A TV won't fit, so lay it flat across the cart's top. Your child can grab it from below to hold it in place in case anybody tries to steal it. This will also provide your kid with protection from above, making them totally impervious to attack. You secured the TV and you kept your child safe in a mobile fortress. You're a better parent than you thought.

Make sure your child holds the TV tightly all the way through the checkout line. Relaxing for even a second could cost you the best deal ever. This vigilance should continue once you're back in your own home. Somebody could break in and steal it at any time. Remain permanently on guard with your child. To the untrained observer it might look like you're just vegging out, but really you're taking a patriotic stand for personal property rights. You're not a couch potato; you're a vigilant defender. The watch is yours.

Most Useful Things to Buy on Black Friday

Item	Why It's Useful
TV	Doubles as a shield against other shoppers.
Sports Gear	Extra armor to make it through the checkout aisle.
Towels	Good for binding wounds.
Mountain Bike	Useful if you need to make a quick escape.
Groceries	Won't be on sale, but will keep you from starving if the battle becomes a siege.
Video Game Console	Can be bartered in exchange for prisoners of war.
Camping Gear	Lets you stake out a position for next Black Friday.
Gift Certificate	Maybe shopping isn't really for you.

BOY BAND CONCERTS

It's the news every parent dreads: Your tween wants to go to a boy band concert. You'll make the usual list of excuses—it costs too much, it's too far away, you'd rather gouge out your eyes with a spoon—but eventually your guilt will get the better of you. You have no reason not to go other than your own preconceived prejudices, which, to be fair, are fully justified. But if your child must undertake this ill-advised misadventure, they might as well do it with you there to protect them. That way, at least they'll have a chance of making it out alive.

But will you survive? According to Dante, boy band concerts are the sixth level of hell, right between the level where everybody in front of you walks too slow and the level where everybody has bad breath and stands too close. (Pro tip: Get buried with mints.) But it's not your immortal soul you'll have to worry about. If you're to the point where you agree to take your child to a boy band concert, your soul is already dead. Nobody who was alive inside would give in that easily. When you get to the concert, you'll notice all the other moms and dads have the same glazed-over look in their eyes that you do. When it comes to parenting, being dead inside isn't a shortcoming; it's a job requirement.

It's not that the music is bad. I mean, it is, but you're going to think that about any music that came out after you were a teenager, just like all the generations before you. Don't open your mind to new music. Instead, embrace hate like a life raft. It's your only chance not to drown in teen hormones. Gross.

To get your child into and out of the concert alive, keep them close. If possible, put a hand on their shoulder. They'll think it's there to reassure them, but really it's to constantly remind them they're there with the least cool person on the planet: you. Anything you do to take them out of their moment will decrease their odds of getting swept up in deadly music mania. A teen concert is just a riot with better rhythm. Having your hand on your kid's shoulder will also let you pull them back when the throngs of amped-up teenagers devolve into a crazed mob. If you think teens are bad when they're lazy, you should see them when they're active. Bring a stun gun.

You'll also need ear protection. Otherwise, the standard concert volumes will blow out your eardrums. Worse, your brain might melt. It's hard for an adult to withstand lyrics written for children ages twelve to fifteen. Rather than trying to make sense of the words, your brain will simply self-destruct—and you'll be grateful. Some things are too dumb for conscious thought.

Parents whose brains melt are the lucky ones. In the worst-case scenario, you'll listen to the boy band music and actually like it. But this mild pleasure will give way to horror as you realize that song will never, ever leave your head. Commit yourself to the nearest asylum. Don't worry, your kid won't be too inconvenienced by your permanent absence from their life. Instead of ignoring you face-to-face, they'll just ignore you from a distance.

If you can't get the necessary ear protection, listen to your own music with earbuds. You'll have to turn it up very loud to compete with the deafening lyrics coming from the stage, but your eardrums are up to the challenge.

And if they're not, it's better to go deaf than to listen to a full boy band set. You'll thank me when you realize it means never again having to hear that one song that literally goes "la la la" because words are hard. Come on, you know the song. Don't make me hum it.

Be sure to take your tween out of the moment whenever possible. When they become enamored with the people onstage, loudly ask, "What do you think that boy's parents do for a living?" or "When do you think was the last time he pooped his pants?" If you keep it up, your child will have a miserable time. With luck, you'll ruin boy band concerts for your kid forever. With less luck, you'll just ruin their relationship with you. That's a risk you'll have to take.

No matter how much your child hates you now, they'll appreciate your sacrifice when they have a child of their own. Then it will be their turn to protect their own kids from the next generation of boy bands. Like mythical monsters that return every few decades, a new generation of teen singers will rise up to threaten the earth. Do your part and ruin concerts for your child now. The world will thank you.

CLOWNS

You might wonder why clowns are in this section rather than the supernatural one. While there are undoubtedly some clowns who possess demonic powers, most of the clowns who fill our collective nightmares are just regular people in makeup. That makes them even scarier. All it takes to become a clown is some face paint and an insatiable desire to murder children. And, yes, I realize not all clowns kill kids. Some just abduct them and turn them into slaves in their secret clown workshops. What do they manufacture? I have no idea. If you want to know, get yourself abducted.

To keep your children safe, avoid natural clown habitats. Regular clowns hang out at circuses, while supernatural clowns dwell in sewers. It can be hard to tell the difference since both places smell the same. Also be on guard at carnivals, in the woods, in the dark, in the light, any time you're alone, and any time you're with other people. Basically, be on the lookout for clowns all the time no matter what. It's not like you had anything better to do.

So how can you defend your child against clowns? First, encourage your kid to have a healthy level of clown phobia. Put on a clown mask and jump out at your kid at random times, like when they're taking a shower or sleeping. You want them to be constantly terrified that a clown could come at them out of nowhere. That's an accurate simulation of real life.

If your child does encounter a real clown, make sure they know what to do. If your kid is with a group of other children, train them to designate one kid to confront the clown head-on while the other kids escape. That child should be the one the other kids like the least and definitely not one of their family members. No clique is complete without someone expendable. If your child is by themselves or cornered, teach them to fight back. The best weapon is water. If they throw it in the clown's face, it will wash the clown's makeup into its eyes, blinding it. Then have your kid set the clown on fire. It's the polite thing to do.

Until the government institutes nationwide clown control, you'll have to depend on this kind of vigilante justice to keep the clown population in check. But remember that you can't just go around hurting people, even when those people put on demonic makeup to scare the hell out of you. They actually have to be a threat to you or your child in that moment before you can take action. If a clown actively tries to abduct your kid, you're in the clear to solve your problems with fire. But if a creepy clown is just walking down the street minding its own business, keep your distance. The best way to keep your child safe from a clown is to let it continue on its way to kill somebody else.

Scariest Types of Clowns

Type of Clown	Why It's Scary
Whiteface Clown	Goes way too heavy on the foundation.
Auguste Clown	Feigned incompetence hides real proficiency with an ax.
Tramp Clown	Hangs out outside the liquor store, blocking you from booze.
Sad Clown	Makes you feel sorry for it before it murders you.
Clown Mime	Silent death.
Rodeo Clown	Turns your future burgers against you.
Jester	Makes despots laugh, extending their life spans.

EMPLOYMENT

Someday, a terrible tragedy will befall your child: They'll get a job. This fate is unavoidable, unless you want them to live with you forever. One of the main goals of parenting is to get your child to stop mooching off of you. But that doesn't make employment any less of a threat to your child's well-being.

A job might not kill your kid, but it will certainly crush their will to live. Just look what happened to you.

To be clear, I'm not talking about jobs that are actually dangerous. Forget coal mining or serving in the military. While those are fine professions, I have no advice for jobs that pose actual, physical threats to life and limb. This book can only protect them from jobs that are dangerous on a mental or emotional level. These forms of employment are especially prevalent in a child's teenage years. A kid's first job is seldom as a CEO with a seven-figure salary. Instead, they start out working the worst jobs imaginable for minimum wage. That kind of work might convince your kid that employment is a scam. If you're not careful, you'll end up with a jobless communist. Unless you want to spend every Thanksgiving getting lectured about the merits of Che Guevara, act now to help your child survive unbearable entry-level employment.

You might think the challenges of minimum-wage jobs vary greatly, but they're more or less the same. Whether you work in data entry, fast food, or galactic bounty hunting, the monotony is universal. The greatest challenge will be convincing your child to care about something that barely pays them enough to cover the cost of gas to drive there. As a white-collar worker for most of my life, I can attest that I seldom cared about my work, even when I was paid fairly. If I were ever underpaid, I would have reached a level of apathy so extreme, it would have been like dividing by zero. If you want to see what would happen if the earth were crushed in a black hole of indifference, cut my pay by a little.

To make your child care about work, offer additional nonmonetary incentives. Before your child goes off to work, give them a pep talk about the importance of labor in the free market. Then promise to never give them that lecture again as long as they stay at their job. Your sound advice will be the stick, and your silence will be the carrot. There's no greater motivating force in the world.

You can also offer minimal economic assistance to make your child's minimum-wage job go further. Subsidize their car by helping to pay for their insurance and gas. Your kid can't work if they can't afford to get there.

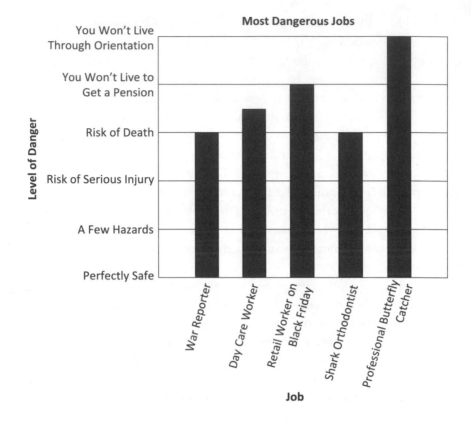

The last thing you want is for them to be stranded in your house. And the sooner they get to work, the sooner they can rise through the ranks to an equally soul-crushing but slightly better-paying job. And that makes it all worthwhile. At least for you, since they'll finally have enough money to cover their own bills.

If your child gets discouraged by the depressing, repetitive nature of their work, reassure them about what lies ahead. Work will always suck, no matter what they do. It's just that at some point, it will suck in a way that doesn't make them smell like French fries. Tell them not to give up because there's literally nothing else to look forward to. But if they don't get back out there, you'll give them that lecture again. That threat never gets old.

MUGGING

You're walking down a dark alley with your kid. I don't know why. Maybe you just like dark alleys, or perhaps your kid wanted to see the spot where Bruce Wayne's parents were murdered. That's not ominous at all.

To the surprise of no one, an unsavory character steps out from behind a dumpster. That's a totally normal place for a person to hang out.

"Give me all your money," they say.

What should you do?

Laugh. You have a kid. You don't have any money. You spent it all on day care and school and vaccinations and the stupid toy from that one commercial they just had to have but never actually played with. Keep laughing. Now it's creepy. The mugger slowly backs away. Laugh harder.

"Just leave me alone," the mugger says. Your laughter is now out of control. You're even scaring yourself. Are you insane? Of course you are. You're a parent.

"Just take it," the mugger says. They throw their own wallet at you and run away.

Don't pursue them. You have their identifying information. Ruin their credit. Ruin their relationships. Ruin their life.

Will a mugging in front of your kid actually play out this way? Yes, every single time. That's why muggers are naturally afraid of parents. If only Bruce Wayne's mom and dad knew how to laugh.

PIRATES

It's a typical day at the park with your kid. The sun is shining, the birds are chirping, and the pirates are launching a surprise attack. Bummer. I don't mean modern pirates in speedboats who hijack cargo ships for ransom. Tom Hanks already dealt with all of them. He's the captain now. The pirates in the park are the old-timey kind in a wooden ship with masts and sails and a black flag with a skull and crossbones, but in the present day. Anachronistic? Maybe. A threat to your child? Without a doubt. People might not talk about pirates much anymore, but there's no proof they all died out. Nobody ever did a head count.

The pirate ship in question is anchored in a small duck pond in the middle of the park. Why is the pirate ship there? Why is anything anywhere? Stop asking questions. The pirates fire an opening volley from their cannons as a raiding party shambles down the nets toward their landing boats. What should you do?

First, tell your kid to stop feeding the ducks. Avian nutrition is important, but not as important as your child's life. Also, maybe the pirates are just protecting the ducks from overfeeding. Even high-seas bandits have hearts.

Next, prepare for battle. If you make a mad dash for your vehicle, you're sure to be cut down by cannonballs, so engage the pirates on foot instead. Get in close so they can't fire their cannons without taking out their own people. Position your child behind you so they'll be shielded from the pirates' initial attack, but let your kid know that you expect them to jump out to trip anyone with a wooden leg. It's the one and only time it's okay to exploit someone's disability.

Pull a swashbuckling sword out of your diaper bag. Not carrying a diaper bag? Pull a swashbuckling sword from your purse or fanny pack. Not carrying a swashbuckling sword at all? Clearly we pack very differently. Check any bags you do have to see what other weapons you have available. If your child is young enough to need a diaper bag, you might have diaper cream. Squirt it at a nearby pirate, preferably one with an eye patch. With one eye missing and the other eye covered by butt paste, they'll be out of the fight. One pirate down, an entire crew to go.

If you see a pirate with a hook, use the handles on your bag to snag it and topple the pirate. It shouldn't be hard. People with eye patches, hooks,

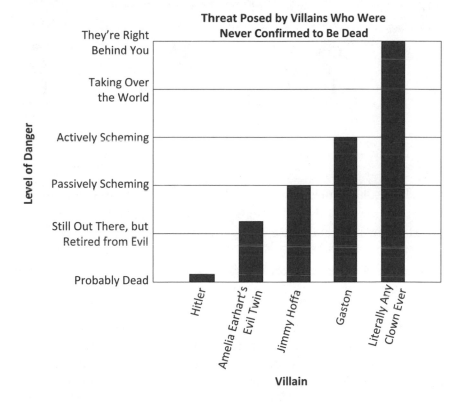

and wooden legs aren't the best fighters. If they were, they'd still have their original body parts. There's a school of thought that says most pirates actually had two eyes and that the eye patches were just to help with dark vision when they went below deck. But those "experts" have never seen a pirate ship in a duck pond, so you can ignore them. Nobody knows more about pirates than you.

Once the pirates are defeated, make a hasty retreat. You don't want the pirates still aboard the ship to realize they have a clear shot with their cannons. Get in your vehicle and peel out of the parking lot. Never return, and never let your guard down at a duck pond again.

REAL-LIFE MUSICAL

Musicals look like a dream onstage, but if you're caught inside one, they're a living nightmare. This is doubly true if you're with your kid. Everyone around you will sing and dance with perfect choreography, while you stand there, scared and bewildered. You'll be singled out immediately for not knowing the words and moves, and both you and your child will become outcasts. Or bigger outcasts than usual.

How can you survive the most rhythmic of all dystopias? First, figure out if you're actually in a musical or just stuck in line to audition for *American Idol*. There are a few key differences. If you're queued up for the reality show, the singing will be sad, desperate, and off key, but if you're living in a musical, the singing will be menacingly harmonious. There are other ways to tell if you're in the middle of a musical apocalypse. Do total strangers resolve their conflicts with perfectly timed song-and-dance numbers? Are everyone's faces heavily caked with stage makeup? Are people projecting their voices with unnecessary volume toward an unseen audience? If the answer to any of these questions is "yes," you're trapped inside a real-life musical. Don't panic. That will only throw off your singing voice.

Next, find out if there were rehearsals. Training an entire population to sing and dance together requires months of intense practice. Where were you? Stupid question. You were busy raising your kid. At times you were only vaguely aware the outside world existed. Of course you missed the notices nailed to your door that said you needed to show up at practice under penalty of torture. Honestly, you were locked inside with your kid. There's no torture worse than that.

After you verify that you did in fact miss the practices, figure out if you can fake your way through the musical. As the central players dance and sing their hearts out in the spotlight, try to be one of the background characters who just snaps in time or sings backup vocals. As a parent, you should always avoid the big parts. The more attention you bring to yourself, the more attention you'll bring to your child. Then you'll never be able to fake your way out of this, especially if your kid opens their mouth. They're bound to say—or sing—something that gives you away. The best lie is saying nothing at all.

If calling attention to your kid can't be avoided and they're under the age of eight, dress them up like a teddy bear. Then it won't matter what they're actually supposed to do in the real-life musical. They'll be cute, and everybody will go "aww" and leave them alone. If your child insists on a speaking role (and when has a child not insisted on speaking?), you'll have your work cut out for you. Understand that every snide or whiny comment your kid makes will elicit a full song-and-dance number from the rest of the cast. Is your child prepared to have an entire musical thrown back in their face? If not, encourage them to be quiet for the first time in their life. If they're ready for it, though, sit back as they speak their mind. For once, it won't be your job to put them in their place. It takes a village to deliver the ultimate lyrical burn.

Obviously, you can't fake your way through the musical forever. At some point, you'll have to escape. Good luck getting out. If there's one thing the theater crowd hates, it's an early exit. Your best bet is to say something emotional and controversial to kick off a high-conflict, high-volume show tune. Then wait beside your human teddy bear as the actors go all-out singing and dancing their arguments for why you're wrong. When they finish, they'll stand there, breathing heavily, waiting for applause. That's when you make your break for it. They'll be too winded to chase you.

Take your child to another city. If that city is also overrun with song and dance, keep going. It's easier than sticking around and learning new lines and dance moves. You don't have time for that. You have a kid. If the entire world is overrun by the drama department, set up a shack in the desert and ride out the world's most lyrically satisfying apocalypse. Eventually, everyone else will sing and dance themselves to death, and you and your kid will be left to rebuild society on your own. You can do it. Just make sure you take off your child's teddy bear costume first. The new ruler of the wastelands should be intimidating, not relentlessly adorable.

RIOTS

There's nothing more human than assembling in a large group to be violent just because. You don't need a good reason for a riot. In fact, if you have a good reason, it's not a riot at all. It's a civic demonstration, and those waste perfectly good destructive energy by making the world a better place. Riots are pointless destruction for the sake of destruction. In other words, it's what your kid does every day.

As a parent, your challenge is both to protect your kid from the riot and to prevent them from joining it. Kids need little motivation to throw in with a group that's already destroying everything. It's every child's dream. No matter how hard you try to get your kid to join the chess club or that charity for deaf kittens, they'll always drift toward angry mobs instead. This is probably your fault. It was a mistake to get them that crowbar for Christmas.

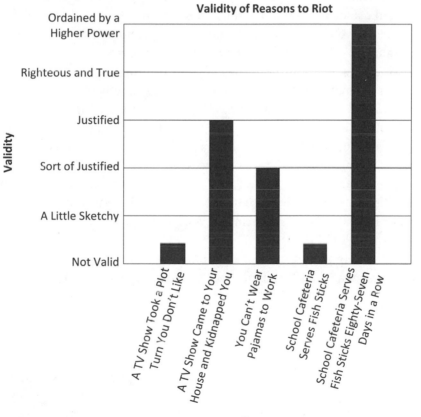

To keep your child from being hurt or hurting others, stay alert for the early warning signs of a riot. Ask yourself these key questions: Are large numbers of people milling about for absolutely no reason? Are they holding torches and pitchforks? Is there something that might spark them to anger? If the city council recently took an official position on the right way to pronounce "GIF," it might be a good time to barricade your doors and never go outside again. Unless you pronounce it differently than me. Then you deserve to be swept up in the destruction.

If you get caught in a riot and your child is small, pick them up to protect them from the angry masses. If your kid is bigger than you, get behind them and use them as a human shield. It's time for them to give back for a change. Push your way through the rioting crowd and try not to breathe too deep. You'll thank me when the police launch tear gas.

Avoid personal property damage by not having nice things in the first place. As a parent, you should be way ahead of the game on that. Chances are, if you did have expensive things, your kids destroyed them years ago. Think of that as a preventive measure, like when firefighters burn a small area of forest to create a break to stop a bigger forest fire. By trashing your home and your vehicle on a small scale, your child is protecting you from the bigger riots to come. Rioters will pass by your house without causing any additional damage because it will already look destroyed. Be grateful for your kid's affinity for mayhem, but not out loud. Otherwise they'll take it as an invitation.

That's really all it takes to save yourself and your child from every kind of riot. Except a Quiet Riot. Refer back to the concert section for them.

WAR

You're walking down the street with your kid when the Canadian army invades. I don't know why. This is a book about parenting, not US–Canada relations. But most of the time in Canada, it's too cold to go outside, so people just sit indoors nursing grudges. They're still bitter about that one time we beat them at curling.

If the Canadian army caught you off guard, it means one of two things: The Canadians moved with record-breaking speed, or you're extremely unobservant. As a fellow parent, I can't blame you for not watching the news. All it does is make you feel worse about everything. It's the opposite of alcohol. Either way, one minute you're telling your child not to eat a rock they found on the ground, and the next you're watching Canadian shock troops storm your town. I'll bet you a toonie you didn't see that coming.

Keeping your child safe in a war zone could be challenging. The point of war is to make people not be alive anymore, which is the opposite of your goal for your kid. But you're not totally unprepared. Raising a child is like being at war for eighteen straight years. You're surrounded by rubble, there are loud noises everywhere, and you feel drained and defeated, even when you win. War might be more relaxing.

Once you notice the Canadians have invaded, figure out where the enemy soldiers are so you and your child can be literally anywhere else. Don't worry about keeping your child quiet as you retreat. War is one of the few things louder than they are. But don't tell your kid that. They might take it as a challenge.

As you move, be mindful of the differences between the Canadian army and every other fighting force in the world. The Canadian army is polite, even when killing you. The side of every bullet is engraved with "Sorry." Canadian soldiers also ride into battle on a moose. That's moose, singular. His name is Bert, and he's a force to be reckoned with. Finally, instead of diesel, the Canadian military runs on maple syrup. This includes the moose. If you see Bert chugging a bottle, back away. He's powered up and ready for war.

As the conflict unfolds, don't let your child join an insurgent group to fight back against the Canadians. That didn't end well for the teens in *Red Dawn*. Besides, chances are the Canadians will eventually leave on their own, apologizing the whole way.

To beat the Canadians while keeping your child safe, take a page from the Russian playbook. Napoleon and Hitler were both defeated at least in part by winter. This time, the American summer will carry the day. The Canadian summer is two weeks long and only warm enough for Canadians to switch from their heavy parkas to their light ones. The American summer, on the other hand, makes water burst into flames. Simply find some place with air-conditioning for you and your child to hole up in. Come July or August, the Canadian army will either run away or melt. It's not their fault. Half of them are snowmen.

Use the time you're locked down with your kid to get to know them better. Ask what their favorite animal is. If they say a moose, denounce them as a traitor. Always be on the lookout for spies, even in your own family.

When the Canadian army finally retreats, celebrate with your kid, but not too hard. You may have kept your kid alive, but you didn't help your country. Congratulations on doing literally nothing to drive out the Canadian scourge. The best patriotism is the kind where other people do the heavy lifting.

HUG IT OUT

With careful planning, your child can survive the threat posed by any human, even you. If children were truly fragile, mediocre parenting would have wiped us off the earth centuries ago. But we're still here, and we're not going anywhere. If anything, humans have become too good at surviving other humans, thanks in no small part to this chapter. I just helped to over-crowd the earth.

Really, the danger posed by other people is nothing compared to the threat your child poses to themselves. And even though they're with them-selves twenty-four hours a day, seven days a week, most kids still make it to adulthood. Trust the statistics and your kid will probably be okay. Your child isn't special enough to be an anomaly.

Still, for extra insurance, keep these dos and don'ts in mind:

✘ **Don't** assume someone is human just because they look like it from a distance. You never know when you might run into a doppelgänger at a frozen research base.

✓ **Do** be suspicious of all human beings, except Mister Rogers. Actually, be extra suspicious of Mister Rogers, if you see him walking around. He's supposed to be dead.

✘ **Don't** let everyone else know you suspect them. You'll just tip off the Canadian spies hiding in our midst.

✓ **Do** teach your child that strangers are dangerous.

✘ **Don't** remind them that deep down we're all strangers, even to ourselves.

✓ **Do** keep in mind that humans are still pretty great when compared to other intelligent creatures, like dwarves or elves. Remember where your loyalties lie.

✗ **Don't** forget you possess the same weaknesses as other humans. You can still die from bullets, bombs, and asteroid strikes, no matter how many days in a row you remember to take your vitamins.

✓ **Do** buy a dog. Or a pig. Those are way safer than humans.

If you stick to the guidelines laid out in this chapter, you'll be ready to protect your kid from other people. It's so easy, a human could do it.

CHAPTER 5

PUBLIC PROBLEMS

Given the dangers posed by other human beings, it might seem safer to avoid them altogether. That's because it actually would be safer. The key to immortality is to live alone. Unfortunately, you gave up your chance at total isolation when you had a kid. You and your child will be required to leave the house and encounter other people at a mind-boggling number of public functions to fulfill school and other social obligations. To get through them in one piece, you'll have to work together, or at least work less against each other than normal. Nobody actually wants to go to these things, least of all your child. Show them you're on their side by being equally miserable.

Unfortunately, your unhappiness will just make your job harder. As a parent, you're still required to protect your child from all dangers, which in this case will be mental and emotional as well as physical. Death by embarrassment is real, at least according to every teenager ever. That's why your kid still asks you to drop them off a block from their school rather than pulling up in front of their friends in your minivan. Make your kid walk to save a life.

PLAYDATES

Avoid playdates at all costs. They almost always become an awkward, platonic double date where the kid and their parent both stay the whole time as a package deal. That means while your child is making a friend, you'll have to make a friend, too. If you're old enough to be a parent, you're too old to upgrade any platonic relationship past the loose acquaintance stage. It's not that you can't. It's just that you'd rather do literally anything else. You sign up for a social call, but what you get is a torture session. Skip the small talk and opt for the rack.

Be prepared for an entire afternoon of uncomfortable silences. The only thing you have in common with the other kid's parent is you both reproduced. That's not exactly a great conversation topic.

As for kids, everything is more dangerous on a playdate. Your child will play fast and loose with the rules to impress their new friend or possibly just to abuse their new friend's toys, if the friend brought any with them. It's like when you rent a car. You only have it for the day, so you use the hell out of it. Expect to hear cracking plastic and a lot of crying. Keep your kid's door closed and cross your fingers that whoever got hurt can walk it off.

If you're lucky, your child will only hurt themselves. If you're not so lucky, they'll hurt the other child. Then you'll have the unpleasant duty of either disciplining your child and apologizing on their behalf or doubling down and blaming the other kid while that kid's parent is right there. To minimize this awkwardness, I recommend holding playdates at a neutral location like a bowling alley or park, as long as there aren't any geese. That way, if somebody gets hurt, they can't sue you and take your house. Although they might still try. The law favors whoever has the more expensive lawyer.

In general, playdates, like all other kinds of dates, just lead to danger and trauma. The best policy is to avoid them altogether. Maybe your child will wait to have friends until they're old enough to drive. Or perhaps they'll wait until they're parents themselves and don't need friends. Either way, don't feel forced to socialize your kid too early. "Loner" is just another word for survivor.

BIRTHDAY PARTIES

Children's birthday parties: where parents celebrate another year of their child's life by almost killing them. These parties have too many kids, too much sugar, and possibly too many clowns, which is any number of clowns greater than zero (see chapter four). It's also a complex, rapidly evolving social situation with few clues for how you or your child should proceed. There's little to like about a child's birthday party, except the cake. If possible, just eat as much of it as you can and then run away into the woods, never to be seen again. Short of that, here's what to do.

First, if you're supposed to attend some other kid's birthday party, evaluate whether or not your child will even remember it. If your kid is still a toddler, you can skip the party and your child will never know the difference. If the parents of the other kid ask where you were, say the invitation got lost in the mail. Better yet, never go anyplace other parents can question you. In fact, don't show up anywhere ever again. Withdraw from society and erase any trace you ever existed. The woods are still calling.

If you do get stuck attending a birthday party for someone else's kid, show up with a gift and your child. If you forget either of those two things, the situation will get awkward fast. When you arrive at the party, glance around to see if other parents are staying. If all the other moms and dads are still there, you're stuck for what will probably be the most painful time of your life—unless you've ever been in labor. Then it will be a close second. If you're supposed to stay, don't dump your kid and run. If you leave, somebody else will dump their child on you at your kid's next party. Karma is whiny and puked in the bounce house.

During all of this, you'll be forced to make awkward small talk with other parents. If you don't, you'll be the creepy person in the corner. Then, instead of painfully conversing with other parents, you'll end up talking with the police. To avoid the legal system, here are some excellent ice breakers to use with other parents: "You can tell just by looking which kids were delivered vaginally." "Does this look infectious to you?" "Do you also wake up every morning and just scream?" After using these conversation starters, people will leave you alone without calling the authorities. Well done.

There are other threats at the party beyond the awkwardness of being there. Most of these come in the form of other kids. If your child claims the piece of cake with the most frosting, the party could devolve into a *Lord of the Flies* situation. Tell your child to wait their turn and to let the birthday kid take the best slice. Etiquette demands it if you want your child to live.

Most birthday parties end right after the cake. Other parents want to sugar up your kid and then ship them back to your house as quickly as possible. This is pure evil, and the other parents know it. Most birthday parties aren't done for a child's benefit, but to retaliate against some other parent who similarly wronged their peers with a cake-and-run. Break the cycle by not throwing a birthday party for your child. That won't work because your parental guilt will overwhelm you, but you can still fantasize about it as you spend six weeks picking out the theme for when your child turns two.

The Most Evil Gifts to Buy for Someone Else's Kid

Gift	Why It's Evil
Drum Set	Peace and quiet were rare before. Now, they'll be extinct.
A Whistle	All the noise of drums but none of the space concerns. Their kid can be awful anywhere.
Puppy	A decades-long obligation the other parent can't give up without making their kid hate them.
Fireworks	They have to buy their kid specialty gloves due to a sudden shortage of fingers.
Real Sword	The sword is free. The emergency room visits cost extra.
Permanent Markers	Permanent damage.
Water Gun	There will be water everywhere in their bathroom but the bathtub.
Ouija Board	Why beat around the bush with evil when you could have evil's direct extension?

NEIGHBORHOOD COOKOUTS

As far as dangers go, a neighborhood cookout isn't the worst place in the world. At least death comes with a side of grilled meat.

You might wonder what could possibly harm your child at a neighborhood cookout. After all, backyards are supposed to be the perfect play spaces for kids. That's the problem. Kids congregate in backyards, and two kids are half as smart as one kid. Get a whole pack of them together and there won't be a functioning brain cell among them. That's when the real fun begins. Minor risks build into bigger risks, which build into visits to the emergency room—or the morgue, depending on just how high they climbed on the roof before they jumped off. In their defense, they would have won two dollars if they'd pulled off that triple backflip.

Monitor the roving packs of kids as best you can while keeping a close eye on the grilled meats, which are obviously your top priority. To succeed, you'll have to stay sharp. I'm not saying you can't drink. In fact, there's almost no way to survive interacting with neighbors without the aid of alcohol. I'm just saying don't drink so much that you don't notice when the roof jumpers set up a judge's table. Otherwise, if (actually, when) your kid hurts themselves, you'll need a designated driver to the hospital. Those are called EMTs, and the ambulance trip will be the most expensive chauffeured ride of your life.

The grill itself also poses a risk. With children zipping around, it's only a matter of time until someone runs into it. This might not seem likely. In fact, I don't know of a single child who's ever run into a grill—except for me. My grandparents had a small grill that was low to the ground. One day, I was walking backward and fell over it while it was still red hot, severely burning the backs of my legs. What was going through my head when I decided to walk backward near a red-hot grill? I don't know. There were other kids around, so obviously I couldn't think.

Your kid should be fine if you keep an eye on them and the meat while you slowly nurse your beer. But maybe move the grill just in case.

FAMILY REUNIONS

One of the downsides of having a kid is other people want to see them. Even worse, some of those people will be related to you. Every few years, your relatives want to find out firsthand what you've done with your life. Since you're likely a professional and personal disappointment, they'll focus on your kid. At least you didn't screw up the continuation of the family's bloodline. Yet.

Your main goal at a family reunion is to seem like you have your act together until the earliest possible moment when it's socially acceptable to leave. This will be your relatives' only direct information on you for months or possibly years, and you want to leave them with a positive impression. This makes it more likely they'll mention you in their wills, or at least less likely they'll spread malicious gossip about you. Your reputation doesn't matter until you need a relative to babysit your kid for free. Then your good name is worth fifteen dollars an hour plus the cost of pizza.

To make the best possible impression, dress your child in something nice. Just don't pick something too nice, because whatever they put on will be filthy in a matter of moments. This is true even if the event is at a clean indoor venue. If the event is outdoors, your child will come back to you covered in mud, even if it hasn't rained in the last half century. Your relatives are unlikely to babysit for you in the future if they think you're raising a swamp monster. Bring diaper wipes.

Besides mud, the other constant at any family reunion is a potluck. Your relatives will judge you as a parent and provider based on what you bring. I recommend buying a dessert at the store. This won't give your relatives any measurable data on you, but they won't care because the dessert will be delicious. Everything's better when it's not made by you.

When you go through the line for the food table, let your kid pack their plate with desserts. Elderly relatives love letting other people's kids ingest dangerous levels of sugar. By letting your kid indulge, you'll win literal brownie points you can use toward future childcare. Plus that dessert pile will make it more likely your kid will look forward to seeing those distant relatives and won't leave them tied to a chair if they ever come over to babysit. Be proactive to keep hostage situations to a minimum.

What the Item You Brought to Your Family Potluck Says About You

What You Brought	What It Says About You
Vegetables	You hate your family.
Casserole	You love your family enough to give them your time but not enough to make something they actually like.
Cake	You are everybody's favorite relative.
Pie	You will never be number one.
Jell-O	You remembered this was a potluck last night.

Anything Store-Bought	You remembered it was a potluck on the way to the potluck.
Napkins	You don't want to be invited back.
Yourself	You want to be kicked out.

WEDDINGS

You might think there are only two lives being ruined at a marriage ceremony, but it could easily be three. Protect your child to prevent what starts as a wedding from ending as a funeral.

At most weddings, the greatest threat to your child is the bride. The reason her eyes are so bright is they can literally shoot lasers. She might seem laid back, but you'll find out her true nature when your kid starts running wind sprints up and down the aisle in the middle of the ceremony. You better hope your kid is fast enough to dodge the bride's deadly eye beams. Or you could just keep your child in the pew in the first place, but that would take a wedding day miracle. Be prepared to haul your child out of church at the first sign of trouble. The first sign of trouble is that your child is at the wedding. They don't want to sit in a hot, stuffy room where boring people perform a boring ceremony with boring words. Their desire to leave is completely rational, but if you're stuck there, so are they. Make sure they suffer in silence. The last thing you want is for the audio in the wedding video to be just your kid screaming.

Things get more dangerous for everyone when the bride and groom leave the church. If the couple lets you throw rice, expect your kid to suddenly throw fastballs like they pitch for the Yankees. Warn the bride and groom to shield their faces unless they want to go on their honeymoon with matching eye patches. That could lead to a deadly misunderstanding if they venture by a duck pond.

The reception hall is just as hazardous. Expect your kid to be drawn to the chocolate fountain like a moth to a flame. Dress your kid in floaties just in case. Nothing kills a party like a kid drowning in chocolate.

On the dance floor, your child will transform again from being at risk to being the risk. Small children dart in and out of the fray, causing pileups like squirrels running through traffic. But the alternative is to let your child run amok among the tables, where they might knock over something even more valuable, like a floral arrangement. It's cheaper to pay someone's medical bills than to replace a wedding centerpiece. Keep your kid on the dance floor and hope that anyone who falls over is too drunk to get hurt. Guardian angels protect those who party properly on a wedding day. It's the one perk of being Catholic.

Leading Causes of Divorce

FUNERALS

Children and funerals go together like peanut butter and turpentine. It's hard to keep your kid alive at a funeral, especially if the funeral is theirs. But let's assume your kid is still alive and someone else is in the coffin. So far, so good.

Everyone is extra sensitive at funerals, so it's the worst possible place to bring a child. Unfortunately, you might not have a choice. If it's a family member's funeral, all your free babysitters will be at the funeral with you. One of them might even be in the casket. Talk about lying down on the job. Also, people might think it's nice to see your child. They're delusional, but those in the throes of grief seldom make the best decisions. In theory, your child is a pleasant reminder that life goes on. In practice, your child's presence is a reminder that hell isn't just in the afterlife.

To keep your child safe at a funeral, keep them away from the casket. Your kid might tip it over and get trapped underneath, which is definitely a risk to their physical well-being. Also, the spirit that used to hang out in that corpse won't exactly be thrilled with your child's behavior. Don't be surprised if your kid gets haunted for all eternity. Keep some holy water handy just in case.

If it's a closed-casket funeral, your child might accidentally lock themselves inside the casket. Sound irrational and unlikely? Welcome to raising a kid. If your child can lock themselves in a trunk, they can lock themselves in a casket. The reason you never hear about incidents like that is because nobody wants to admit they happened. Honey, I buried the kids.

Hold your child's hand when in the receiving line to comfort the bereaved. This will keep your kid close as well as give the illusion of affection you probably don't feel for your child at that particular moment. More likely, you'll be on edge because of the social pressure not to ruin someone's final send-off. Prepare your most subtle death glare to keep your child from asking inappropriate questions. It won't work, but you have to try.

Other specific survival tricks depend on your individual culture. If you're Irish, keep your kid away from the whiskey. If you're in Starfleet, don't let your kid ride the funeral torpedo into space. If you're a Viking, keep your child away from the flaming funeral boat. You don't want to explain to everyone how your kid lost their eyebrows.

PARENT–TEACHER CONFERENCES

Your kid will never willingly tell you what they did at school. Relish this lack of information. It's better not to know what they do when they're gone. But this blissful ignorance will come to an end on one of the most dangerous days of the year. I'm talking, of course, about parent–teacher conferences.

There are risks for both you and your child on conference day. It's dangerous for your kid because you might become so enraged that you disown them. It's dangerous for you because your kid might be falling so far short that their teacher requires you to do extra work with them to help them catch up. Why can't children just raise themselves?

To keep yourself and your child safe, you'll have to strike the right tone from the conference's start. Make eye contact with the teacher, but not in a way that's threatening or domineering. Don't look away. Teachers can sense fear and blood. Double-check your Band-Aids.

Next, sit up straight with a dignified posture to show you're serious. This will be difficult because, if you're at an elementary school, you'll probably be sitting in a tiny child-sized seat. Compensate by hovering in the air mid-squat like you're sitting on a much larger chair. If nothing else, this will prove the power of your leg muscles, which will let the teacher know you mean business. Try not to break a sweat.

As the teacher goes through your child's strengths and weaknesses, maintain a neutral facial expression. The teacher will be unsure if you agree, disagree, or are even listening. They wonder the same things every day about your kid. Without your reassurance, the teacher may be reluctant to make you take corrective action. Nailed it.

To increase your odds of a clean escape, you'll need to make your child behave themselves. That's impossible, so just leave them at home. When the teacher says your kid is disruptive and you disagree, the last thing you need is for your child to knock over three bookshelves like dominos. Kids have a flair for timing.

Ultimately, you and the teacher are on the same team, and have the same goal: making your child just a little better so you can get rid of them for good. The last thing the teacher wants is for your child to repeat a grade, and the last thing you want is for your child to live with you forever. Your kid's teacher is your silent partner, handling all the problems that crop up during normal business hours while you handle nights, weekends, and holidays. Treat the parent–teacher conference as a chance to size up your ally, even if you function as frenemies much of the time. You gain a breather by dumping your kid on the teacher all day, and the teacher regains their sanity by punting them back. After you and the teacher finally meet face-to-face, you'll both sigh heavily and say to yourselves, "That explains so much." And you'll both be right.

What Teacher Comments Actually Mean

Comments	What It Actually Means
They're very energetic.	They're a good candidate for horse tranquilizers.
They're a fast learner.	They spend most of their time bored.
They have an active imagination.	The eyeless people they keep talking about better not be real.
They're my best student.	They don't have much competition.
They have a bright future.	They have a tendency toward arson.
They don't apply themselves.	They apply themselves, but only to evil.
They're very social.	It's illegal for me to tape their mouth shut. I checked.
It's a pleasure to teach them.	I'd quit if I didn't fear starvation.

GRADUATIONS

Sometimes, your kid's entire childhood seems to go by in the blink of an eye. Other times, it comes to a full stop and feels like it will never move forward again. Graduations are one of the latter. The average length of a high school or college commencement ceremony is literally forever. That's a lot of time for you to be on guard against slow-moving but serious threats. If you're not careful, your kid could die of old age right there in the auditorium. Make them update their living will just in case.

The most immediate risk at any graduation is overheating. Your kid will be wearing stifling dress clothes with robes over the top. When robes were invented in the Middle Ages, they weren't designed with ventilation in mind. In fact, they were created for the opposite reason. It was beneficial if your robes kept you from freezing to death in your unheated classroom at the monastery. Now, graduation robes over-insulate your child in a hot gymnasium. Unless you want your kid to melt like a Nazi in *Raiders of the Lost Ark*, you'll need to take active steps to keep them cool.

First, cut ventilation holes in their robes. The garments are long and billowy, so hopefully no one will notice, especially the robe rental company, which will use any excuse to keep your deposit. Or you could strap ice packs all over your child's body. Unfortunately, those warm up quickly and add significant weight. Also, strapping things to your kid's body might teach them the wrong lesson. You don't want your college-bound student to major in drug smuggling. If you must strap ice packs to them, at least use the gel kind, not real ice. If you do, the ice will melt and leave an awkward trail behind your child. That's how stories start.

Another risk you'll have to guard against at the endless graduation ceremony is the moment when your kid walks up the stairs to the stage. They might trip over their robes, making that short stroll their last. To reduce the threat level, lobby for the installation of ramps or possibly an elevator. If all else fails, create a system of pulleys to raise your child to the proper height. This may seem more complex and dangerous than just letting your child walk up the stairs, and it probably is. But at least it will keep your mind and hands occupied during the ceremony, which will last for two hours but feel like two years. I'm sure the graduation speakers won't mind if you operate power tools during their prepared remarks. When your child's name is called, they'll see you've gone the extra mile to get them up on that stage—and be completely horrified. There's no way they'll cross the stage now. If they do, people will realize they're related to you. Although by keeping them off the stage entirely, you'll actually keep them completely safe from tripping on it. Good job by accident, I guess.

How Seriously You Should Take Graduations

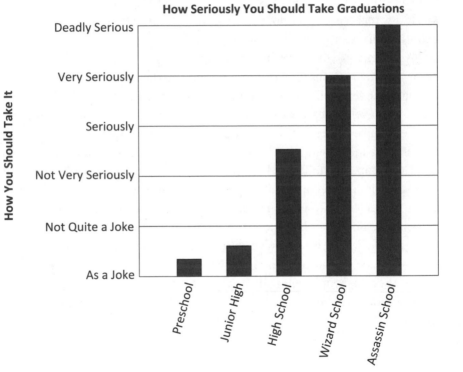

SCHOOL HOLIDAY PAGEANTS

Holiday pageants are just as dangerous as plane crashes but attract less help. The Red Cross won't set up an aid station for your child's all-school performance. Emergency responders lack empathy because your problem is self-inflicted. You're the one who didn't use birth control.

School holiday pageants are different than most other survival scenarios because your kid is the danger that you're trying to survive. That's why people take pictures: not to prove they're proud of their kid, but to show what they lived through as a parent. There are no Purple Hearts for making it through whatever seasonally appropriate holiday pageant you've been forced to attend, but those emotional scars never go away.

Unless you want to document that psychological trauma, there's no reason to take a picture of your kid's pageant. When your child sings in a giant group, they don't demonstrate any creativity or personality. Your kid is just following the same instructions as a huge mass of other kids. Actually, it might be the only time you see your child follow instructions. Maybe that's why so many parents tear up.

The first thing you need to do to survive a pageant is to stay hydrated. Scientists claim the best way is with water, but those scientists have never sat through a Thanksgiving play for grades one through six. The best way to stay hydrated is with alcohol. Yes, those same scientists claim alcohol dehydrates you, but alcohol makes you immune to science. Drink enough and no limits of human physiology can stop you.

Imbibe enough to tune out the scenes onstage but not enough to cause a scene yourself. Schools could solve their fund-raising problems forever if holiday pageants had a cash bar. Unfortunately, human decency prevents most bartending services at elementary schools. Instead, you'll have to be your own bartender. There are many ways to sneak in alcohol, the easiest of which is in your stomach. Never underestimate the value of pre-gaming.

If time constraints don't allow you to drink beforehand, you'll have to sneak alcohol into the event. In that case, stick to hard liquor. You want the greatest bang per liquid ounce because weight and space will both be issues.

It's tough to sneak in a case of beer in your pant legs. Unfortunately, hard liquor tastes like hot garbage. Scratch that. It tastes like room-temperature garbage. But even the foulest liquid is better than sobriety. It's a lesson too many parents have learned the hard way.

You obviously can't admit how much you loathe these kind of school events to the people around you, even though they'll all be thinking the same thing. If we admitted that we hate holiday pageants, the pageants would stop forever and civilization would collapse. At least I assume that's

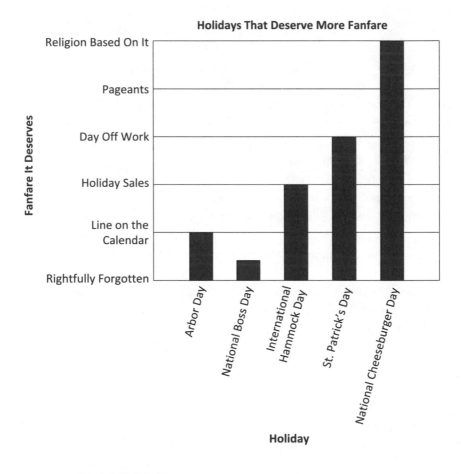

what would happen. Otherwise why would parents would keep torturing themselves like this?

Therefore, you have to keep drinking. Confine your swigs to frequent bathroom breaks or bring a cartoonishly long crazy straw and hide the flask in your coat. You should have a coat on since most pageants are confined to cold-weather months. They're the leading cause of seasonal depression.

With any luck, you'll imbibe enough to survive even the most unbearable holiday pageant. It's your duty to live. No one else wants to raise your kid for you if you die of boredom. You're looking out for the good of society. How unselfish of you.

Top Drinking Days for Parents

Day	Reason It Calls for Drinking
Kid's Birth	First time Mom can drink in forty weeks.
Kid's First Steps	Nothing in your house will be safe again.
Kid's First Words	Baby said "mailman."
Kid's Preschool Graduation	You realize just how many graduations your kid has left to go.
Kid's High School Graduation	One of the last good days before they start racking up college debt.
Kid's First Day of College	You can finally turn their old room into a home gym you'll never use.

Day	Reason It Calls for Drinking
Kid's College Graduation	They're officially no longer your problem. That deserves a toast or nine.
Kid's Wedding Day	You likely paid for the booze. Might as well get your money's worth.

MUSIC RECITALS

When you picture your child in a music recital, you might imagine an angel strumming on a harp. The reality will be more like a demon pounding on a xylophone. Kids aren't great at playing instruments. In fact, kids aren't great at anything, except for doing the opposite of whatever you tell them to do. They're all over that one.

There's a Catch-22 when it comes to your child's musical abilities: The more they practice, the better they'll get. But the more they practice, the more you have to listen to them play their instrument at home. Suffering through their awful play for an hour at a recital twice a year is less painful than listening to it every day in the vain hope they'll get slightly less awful. Take their music teacher's instructions to practice as more of a suggestion than an order. If worse comes to worst, your kid could claim they never heard the teacher in the first place, which is a solid alibi. They're literally holding a noise-making machine that destroys people's hearing.

Discouraging your child from practicing is a great idea right up until it's time for a music recital, which is as inevitable as death and taxes and just as painful. To survive, you'll need heavy-duty ear protection. Regular foam earplugs won't cut it. Your kid is using a tool scientifically designed to make noise. To compensate, you'll need the kind of ear protection normally reserved for shooting ranges. When other parents question you about it, point to your covered ears to show you can't hear them. Assume their scowls are actually expressions of admiration and jealousy. Not everyone can be as awesome as you.

Since you won't hear your kid, you'll have to watch the stage carefully to know when they play. When they're not playing, clap. That means they just finished the song or they haven't started yet. Either way, your child should be encouraged when they're silent. That's when they're at their best.

Once your ears are protected, you'll be better prepared to protect your child. There aren't many threats to a kid at a solo music recital, but if a full band is involved, expect the dangers to be loud and shiny. The most likely scenario is someone in the tuba section will snap and swing their instrument like a bludgeon. You can't blow that much air out of your body without consequences. In the event of a deranged tuba player, charge the stage and grab another instrument to fight them off. I recommend a clarinet. It's straight and hard with one end pointier than the other. Throw it like a javelin. It won't stab anyone, but it might break when you throw it, and that's one less instrument you'll have to listen to later. Then grab your child and run away. Anyone with a tuba will be too slow to follow.

If you're facing a deranged flutist, however, you're in trouble. Tell your child to fight them off with whatever your kid plays. Hopefully, they play an ax. Not a guitar, but a literal chopping instrument. They'll never lose a band fight with that. Plus they can practice at home by chopping firewood. It's both the sharpest and quietest of all the instruments. It's a win-win as long as your kid doesn't accidentally chop off their own arm. Then they'd be demoted to playing the triangle, assuming they can do it one-handed. If they can't, they'll be out of music altogether. Enjoy this rare parenting win and never attend a recital again.

TOO PUBLIC

By using the methods laid out in this chapter, you can keep your child alive through even the most overbooked calendar. While you deal with the unending list of public threats in your life, keep these words of wisdom in mind:

✓ **Do** be honest about your lack of enthusiasm. Fake smiles only encourage future invitations.

✗ **Don't** skip all public events. You have to be selectively absent or people will start knocking on your door to see if you're dead.

✓ **Do** keep a record of when you show up. There's no point in going through the motions if you don't get credit.

✗ **Don't** make your child more social than you have to. Every sport or club they join will be another three dozen times you'll have to leave the house.

✓ **Do** keep your head down. Making accidental eye contact with another parent could trigger unwanted small talk or, worse, accidental friendship.

✗ **Don't** give out your real name and phone number. Sign-in sheets are a trap to recruit volunteers.

✓ **Do** remember it's all about your kid. They're the reason you have to leave the house. Your grudge starts now.

✗ **Don't** become a hermit. That's my dream job. If you do it, too, you'll saturate the market.

By following these pointers, you and your kid will survive public functions, whether you want to or not. Death would be the easy way out. Real parents suck it up and survive, no matter how much it hurts.

CHAPTER 6

DOMESTIC DISASTERS

If going out in public is dangerous, then surely it must be safer to keep your kid home. Sadly, nothing could be further from the truth. Even the most child-proof dwelling still provides twenty or thirty million ways for your kid to hurt themselves. Children have unlimited creativity when it comes to accidental injury. If they had that same imagination when it came to solving problems, we'd have a cure for cancer. But instead, all we have are escalating emergency room bills and never-ending parental headaches. And that's why medical marijuana is legal in most states.

Threats in the home require a different approach than threats outside it. You know to be on guard when you're sitting through a tense PTA meeting or being stalked by a tiger at a roller rink, but you might not be at peak alertness when sitting in your own living room (although you should be if you have a dirty couch). This lack of awareness is only natural. You'd like one place on the planet where you can relax. Instead, you get zero places. Tough luck. You should have thought of that before you reproduced.

In this chapter, I'll explain how to survive some of the most common threats to children inside your own home. Does the presence of these threats make you a bad parent? Yes. But everything makes you a bad parent, at least according to the internet. If everyone is equally awful, then really you're just average. Take pride in that, and focus on keeping your child alive. It's the best you can do.

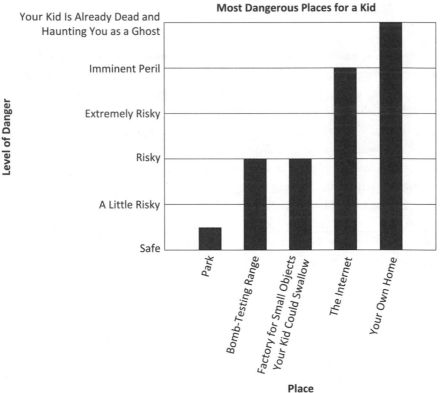

Most Dangerous Places for a Kid

BATHTUBS

Throughout history, the bathtub has been known by many names: the deadly dunk tank, the final-ride slip-and-slide, the porcelain coffin. Parents are acutely aware of the threat it poses—or so they believe. If you think the only danger to your kid is drowning, you underestimate the suicidal creativity of children. Your kid is far more likely to drop a toaster in the bathtub while in it than they are to drown, not because they want to die, but because they want toast. With kids, the more impossible something seems, the more likely it is to happen. Children are the opposite of logic.

Banning kitchen appliances from the bathroom is the first step to keeping your child safe. The next is to fill the tub yourself. Your kid will fight you on this. To a small child, filling the tub is akin to being God. They can flood their village of tiny plastic toys; then the entire bathroom; then the rest of the house. Do not leave the room when your child is near the tub. They're only too eager to test out their divine powers on your floors.

Is a tub really as big of a threat as vampires, ostriches, and all the other extreme dangers in this book? Yes. Not every house has a vampire or an ostrich, but every home has a bathtub. Unless you have a trendy, modern house that only has stand-up showers because you're sure you'll never, ever have kids. Spoiler alert: That's the best way to guarantee you get pregnant.

Shampoo is another danger. Despite its promises to the contrary, children's shampoo is only tear free in the sense that your kid will cry freely when they get it in their eyes. As for soap, it's one of the safest substances ever created, yet children act like it's made of fire. Perhaps it's because children know on a subconscious level that removing the oils that build up on their body could dry out their skin. Or maybe they just oppose anything you want them to do because they're jerks. Either way, your child will reject any cleaning compounds involved in the bathing process. Maybe just spray them with an air freshener and call it a day.

BEDS

Beds are just trampolines with different marketing. When used by children, they both offer the same level of fun—and the same injury rate. What goes up must get a concussion. I think that's how the saying goes.

Even when your child uses their bed correctly, they still might fall out. That's why many parents add safety rails. If customers have to install aftermarket protective equipment to keep their children alive, then your product is inherently dangerous. Yet the FDA still says beds are safe for use by children. Industry insiders have been hiding the real fatality figures for years. Big Pharma has nothing on Big Mattress.

But just because beds are incredibly dangerous doesn't mean you can stop your child from using them. In fact, making your kid sleep on the floor is one of the fastest ways to end up on the news as a terrible parent. Don't expect the media to mention how you totally eliminated the risk of monsters under the bed, either.

In fact, beds are so dangerous that their deadliness has shaped popular music. Remember that song about the monkeys jumping on the bed? Each one falls off and bonks its head. Mama calls the doctor and the doctor says, "Don't bother trying to stop them. They're just going to keep bouncing and falling off." At least that's the way my kids remember it. They're incapable of grasping the song's true message, which is about natural selection. It's not a coincidence that nature now has dozens of monkey species that sleep in trees but none that sleep in beds. But even knowing the dire consequences, the monkeys in the song just keep jumping and falling. In that respect, it's probably the most accurate depiction of child behavior ever written. The only unrealistic part of the song—aside from the fact that the monkeys live in an advanced society where they can both talk and use the telephone—is when the mother consults the doctor after every fall. In real life, no parent would have made that many doctor contacts because each one would have a separate co-pay.

If your child falls off the bed and hits their head, you might wonder if you need to take your kid to the emergency room. You don't. If it were a real emergency, you would know, because you would be on your way to the emergency room instead of wondering if you could keep your kid home to save some money. In a real crisis, your survival genes override your cheapness genes. That's why humans are still around and bed-jumping monkeys are not.

Assuming your genes tell you not to take your child to the emergency room, the main thing you need to do is monitor your kid to see if they throw up because they probably have a concussion. Even then, you don't usually need to take them to the hospital. The physician on call will just tell you to go home and make sure they don't fall asleep for a few hours. This is a bummer because it's not much fun to hang out with a tired, vomiting, concussed child. You might get flashbacks to being the designated driver in college.

In extra-challenging cases, you'll have to figure out if your kid threw up because they're actually concussed or because they ate six pounds of Halloween candy right before they fell. Limits are for quitters. When my wife and I found ourselves in that exact situation with one of our kids, we decided not to go to the hospital and everything was fine. Other than all that wasted Halloween candy.

The Most Dangerous Types of Beds

Bed	Why It's Dangerous
Memory Foam Mattress	Remembers everything. EVERYTHING.
Water Bed	REM sleep works best without the threat of drowning.
Air Mattress	Your back will hurt for a week.
Futon	Your back will hurt for a month.
The Ground	Just stay down there. Your back will never work again.
Bed of Nails	Only slightly more uncomfortable than the ground.
Slay Bed	You probably meant to get a sleigh bed. Fatal mistake.
Flower Bed	What you'll be buried under after the slay bed is done with you.

DOORS

As the saying goes, when God closes a door, he has a good reason, so leave it closed unless you want to unleash the forces of hell upon the earth. I went to Catholic school.

But doors thwart more than demons. They're also the chief temptation and tormentor of children everywhere. Any time two or more kids are in a house together, they'll chase each other, and one kid will slam a door in the other's face. And that's when the game changes from "Catch me if you can" to "YOU SMASHED MY FINGERS." It shouldn't be hard to figure out who lost.

"Don't slam the door!" has been a battle cry of parents everywhere since doors were invented in the late 1980s. Before that, doorways were blocked by strands of dangling beads. It's weird that humans landed on the moon before creating doors, but that's history for you. Neil Armstrong covered the entrance to the lunar module with a tarp.

It's easy to think children might be safer in a home without doors, but doors were actually invented to protect kids. Before doors, children sometimes walked in on things they shouldn't see, which is why the first doors went on master bedrooms. Some nightmares never go away.

Children don't just get their fingers smashed by doors; they also run into them. Doorknobs are the perfect height to clothesline a full-speed toddler. That's why pediatricians recommend kids wear bike helmets at all times until they're five. I disagree. Giving children head protection just leads to more headbutting.

Taller or shorter kids might miss the doorknob but run into the door itself, which is a formidable foe all its own. This could happen for numerous reasons: The lights could be off, your kid could have their eyes closed, or they might be looking behind them as they run away from you. Never warn them in advance that you plan to trim their toenails. But tell your kid not to let down their guard even when the door is open. They might still run into the doorframe, either because they aren't looking or because they're just that clumsy. After all, they did get their hand-eye coordination from you.

So how are children supposed to survive in the Age of Doors? One solution is the open-concept house, which was specifically designed to reduce child mortality rates by eliminating doors. Of course, to get rid of doors, architects had to eliminate walls, too. Pretty soon, an open concept house was just a couch and some beds in the middle of an open field. But look at all that space for entertaining.

Call me a traditionalist, but I don't think we should tear down entire houses just to avoid doors. Maybe it's because I like privacy, or perhaps I'm just not that concerned with whether my kids live to adulthood. Either way, I think it's better to teach children to use doors safely and respectfully rather than to raze all standing structures to the ground and live outside like vagrants. It's probably not worth wiping out society just to protect your kid's precious digits.

To keep your child safe, make sure they only close doors when they have a good reason. Those reasons include:

1. They're wrapping a gift for you.
2. They're being chased by a serial killer.
3. They're pooping.

You can also use these same guidelines for yourself, but be aware that the bathroom excuse won't fly if you have a small child. They'll stand at the door and cry, no matter how much you assure them they do NOT want to see what you're doing in there. Whatever you do, don't open the door. Repel the barbarians at the gate.

Teach your kid to give you plenty of notice when they close a door. If they need to shut one, have them loudly declare their intentions to the entire house, like yelling "Fore!" at the golf course or "Fire in the hole!" in the bathroom. Publicly announcing that you're closing a door is obnoxious and inconvenient, so maybe your kid will just leave their door open in the first place. Or maybe they'll ignore your rule but close the door slowly and stealthily to avoid a fight. Either way, that door will close without any broken fingers or trips to the emergency room. Sounds like paradise to me.

One final thought on doors: Make sure only important doors have locks. Any extra locks beyond the bathroom and master bedroom are an invitation for small children to trap themselves in and you out. Unless you want to chop down doors with a fire ax, keep locks to a minimum. If you do want to chop down doors, don't forget to tell your kid to back up a step or two before you burst through the door like Jack Nicholson. At least you'll know why they have nightmares.

Why is the door locked?

I'm going to the bathroom.

Can you give me a few minutes alone?

No.

Deadliest Doors

Door	Danger It Poses
Garage Door	Death from above
French Doors	Death from both sides
Dutch Door	Death in two halves
Barn Doors	Death in the country
Revolving Door	Death in a circle
Sliding Glass Door	Death you can see through
Pocket Doors	Death tucked away
The Doors	Death by rocking out

Annual Child Fatalities at Home

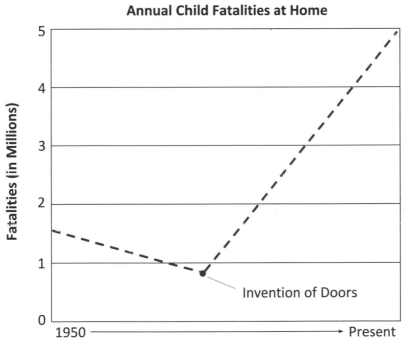

KITCHEN

It's ironic that the room most necessary to keep your kid alive is also the one that's the most likely to kill them. Kids need food to avoid starvation. But food is a choking hazard, a fridge can tip over, and a stove can send your kid to the burn ward. The kitchen is basically a child murder room where you also store your snacks. Keep an eye on the pantry.

It's cliché for kids to touch a hot stove, yet children still do it every year because learning is for cowards. Generation after generation, children manage to ignore obvious warning signs like a red hot coil, a boiling pot of water, or a parent shouting, "Don't touch that! You'll get burned!" If only the message were less subtle. The problem is that touching a hot burner doesn't eliminate anyone from the gene pool, so natural selection doesn't come into play. To stop your kid from hurting themselves, you either have to be vigilant around the stove at all times or let your kid hurt themselves on it so badly they actually die. I recommend the former.

To keep your child safe around a hot stove, establish a buffer zone that keeps them at least an arm's length away. If your child crosses that line, stiff-arm them in the face. Your kid might not learn anything about the dangers of a hot stove, but they'll learn something about football. That's a win, I guess.

Not every child burns themselves in the kitchen. Some accidentally cut themselves instead. I recommend limiting your kid to butter knives. Of course, kids can still cut themselves with butter knives. This isn't because butter knives are sharp, but because people are 80 percent bread. At least some of us are. My normal diet is the opposite of keto.

If you can protect your child against burns and cuts, they should be safe. Just kidding. They might still drink poison. The cabinet under the kitchen sink is full of cleaning solutions that sanitize surfaces by killing all organisms. In a way, I admire our ruthlessness. Human beings would rather destroy all life, our own included, than let the germs take over. We're sure winners and sore losers at the same time.

These chemicals might not kill your child on contact, but they're deadly if ingested. Such a product is too tempting to be protected by a simple child

lock. I recommend not having these chemicals in your house in the first place. Take your chances with the germs. At least that way, if your child gets sick, it'll be because of something microscopic you couldn't see rather than the big bottle of poison you bought on purpose. It's always best to keep things at least one step removed from being your fault. If your kids are going to blame you, at least make them work for it.

MICROWAVE

Most of the dangers in the kitchen have been around for hundreds of years, but modern technology has added a few new, cutting-edge ones worth highlighting. Chief among them is the microwave, which is the closest human beings will ever come to performing magic. It provides near-instantaneous food. Of course, that still isn't fast enough for your kid. That two-minute cook time is somehow long enough for them starve. And when the food is done, your child will still hate it. How dare you pick the wrong flavor of Hot Pocket?

But the microwave isn't just wonderful at irritating your child. It's also dangerous. An adult I know who shall remain nameless once microwaved a bowl of instant macaroni but forgot to add water. The resulting mass of burned pasta and molten plastic slag looked like Satan took a hot dump on a plate. It filled their entire apartment building with fumes, and they had to rush the microwave outside and throw it in the dumpster. And that was one person forgetting one ingredient. Just imagine what your kid could do if they used it to cause damage on purpose.

Monitor your child closely any time they're near the microwave. That is, unless they're older and you told them to feed themselves. By that point, you probably won't be as heavily invested in their survival anyway. But small children should never be allowed to use the microwave. For starters, it might alter their DNA. The only thing scarier than a toddler is a toddler with superpowers. Note: As far as I know, a microwave has never given anyone superpowers or even altered their DNA, but I'm not taking any chances—or doing any research. Facts are for people without microwaves.

Also, it's dangerously easy to turn a simple microwave into a point of ignition. Just add one or two extra zeros to the timer and your helpful appliance will become a volatile firebomb. As a parent, you have to be the microwave time master. Make sure whatever you put in there stays in there for exactly the right interval. A toddler only has to bump the control pad once to turn a forty-second pizza slice into a four-minute Chernobyl. To stay safe, never have leftovers in the first place. The appropriate serving size for pizza is all of it.

Even if your food stays in the microwave for exactly the right amount of time, it will still come out the temperature of the sun. Or it'll still be partially frozen. With microwaves, there's no in-between. Gently test microwaved leftovers with your finger to find out which it is. If your finger hits a solid block of ice, put the food back in the microwave for another minute. If your finger melts off, take a moment to gently blow on the food before serving it to your child. Then watch as your kid rejects the leftovers just like they rejected the food when you cooked it originally. Seriously, why did you think they were left over in the first place?

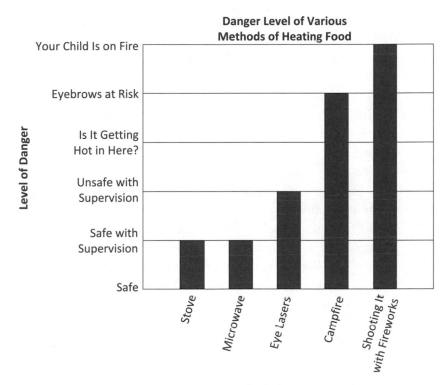

Danger Level of Various Methods of Heating Food

Level of Danger (y-axis), top to bottom: Your Child Is on Fire, Eyebrows at Risk, Is It Getting Hot in Here?, Unsafe with Supervision, Safe with Supervision, Safe

Method of Heating Food (x-axis): Stove, Microwave, Eye Lasers, Campfire, Shooting It with Fireworks

WALK-IN FREEZER

You're locked in a walk-in freezer with your kid. I don't know how you both got trapped, but I can take an educated guess: Your child pulled the door closed behind you because why wouldn't they? If there's any way to make an ordinary situation dangerous, your child will find it. If you learn just one thing from this book, it should be that.

The greater unknown is why you have a walk-in freezer in your house in the first place. That's not exactly standard issue. Maybe you're a chef who tests out new recipes at home. Or maybe you had one installed in the basement because you're a serial killer and need a place to stash the bodies. If that's the case, you probably wouldn't store your family's food in your custom-made serial killer freezer. Never mix business and family.

But for whatever reason, you're in a walk-in freezer now with your kid. And it's not just any walk-in freezer; it's the old kind where there's no way to open it from inside. I don't know why they used to build freezers that way. Maybe they wanted to increase turnover in the restaurant industry. That's one way to cut down on pension costs. But more likely, it's a newer freezer that does have some kind of gadget to open it from the inside, but that gadget is broken. That's just how things work with commercial-grade appliances. Or don't work, I guess.

One of the first things you'll notice when you're locked in a freezer is that it's very cold. Seems kind of obvious. At least the temperature control is working properly. What should you do? I recommend surviving. If your first instinct was to give up and die, you're reading the wrong book.

Assess what tools you have at your disposal. First and foremost is your child. Yes, in the right context, a child can be a tool. In fact, in most contexts, your child is a tool, but the other kind. Use your kid for inspiration. Maybe your parental instincts will kick in and you'll get a rush of adrenaline and superstrength to save your kid. Use it to break through the door like you're an NFL running back playing a grade school team. Or perhaps your child will simply whine so much that you'll be filled with murderous rage, leaving you no choice but to direct that energy at the door rather than at your kid. Life-or-death situations are great therapy.

If you can't knock down the door with your shoulder—which is a distinct possibility since bone isn't as hard as metal even if you drink lots of milk—use the other, non-child tools at your disposal. Peas taste terrible, but at the right velocity a frozen bag of them is as good as an artillery shell. Pick it up and hurl it at the door. If the door breaks, great. And if it doesn't break, well, you just opened lunch. Sit on the peas like you're a chicken hatching an egg. Once they thaw, eat them for sustenance. If the combined taste of peas and your butt doesn't immediately kill you, you'll have the final bit of motivation you need to break out. Even battering yourself to death against a metal door is better than eating vegetables.

If neither your bones nor the vegetables are strong enough to smash through the freezer door, use the metal shelving inside the freezer. First, dismantle it, tearing it apart until it looks like a tornado went through an IKEA store. Focus intently on your child's whining, and you'll be able to bend those metal poles without a problem. Then use the poles to jab holes through the door until it falls off its hinges. But first call out to make sure no one is standing on the other side so that you don't accidentally impale them. Of course, if someone has been standing outside the door this whole time and they didn't open it, they probably deserve to be impaled. Use your best judgment.

Once you leave the freezer, don't forget to take the snacks you went in there to get in the first place. And if you're a serial killer, turn yourself in to the proper authorities. Remember, killing is wrong. Unless you're killing the person who was waiting on the other side of the freezer door without opening it. They had it coming.

WELCOME HOME

Armed with the info in this chapter, you should be able to keep your child alive and more or less intact within the confines of your own house. It's a death trap, but it's your death trap. There's no place like home.

As you fight the good fight, keep these dos and don'ts in mind:

✓ **Do** be on guard at all times in your own home. Relaxation is just a lazy form of suicide.

✗ **Don't** stay awake *all* the time. It's okay to sleep in short bursts as long as you draw eyeballs on your closed eyelids.

✓ **Do** keep a first aid kit in your house. Reattaching an arm yourself will always be cheaper than a trip to the emergency room.

✗ **Don't** read warning labels. There's no point in worrying about any one specific danger when literally everything can kill your kid.

✓ **Do** accept that childproofing your home is an ongoing process. Think of each kid as a booby trap detector. If one child crashes a riding lawn mower through your living room, you'll know what to look out for with the next kid.

✗ **Don't** expect the older kids to catch everything. Your youngest will always find new and exciting ways to almost kill themselves.

✓ **Do** keep trying. Even if it's futile to keep your child completely safe, it's even more dangerous not to try at all.

✗ **Don't** sweat the small stuff. The small stuff can still kill your child, but you need that moisture in your body so you don't get dehydrated.

With that, you know everything you need to keep your child safe in your own home. You won't sleep easy, but you will sleep, even if it's only for a few minutes here or there. As a parent, you have to hope that's enough.

CHAPTER 7

ACCIDENTAL TIME TRAVEL

Throughout this book, I've focused on plausible, real-world survival scenarios for you and your child. This chapter is no exception. Let's talk about time travel.

You now know there's nowhere in the present time that's safe, either standing still or on the move, but what about in the past? Or the future? Your kid will still be in mortal peril whenever you go on the timeline, but the stakes will be higher. It's hard to feel bad about ruining the future since you're setting that in motion right now by living in the present, but the past is a different story. As you try to save your kid in bygone eras, you could accidentally change history. The entire course of human events could be in your hands. What should you do?

Pop culture would have you believe that you shouldn't change anything or the timeline will be altered forever. That's a lie told by rich and powerful people who don't want you to threaten the status quo. For all you know, those elites already could have gone back in time and changed history in their favor. Trust no one.

If you go back in time, change whatever you need to in order to survive—and thrive. Invest in stocks. Bet on sports. Play the lottery. It's possible your meddling could make the world a better place—or destroy it outright. Either way, it's worth it if your family comes out personally enriched. Nobody remembers how many world wars there were supposed to be anyway.

The following are the time travel predicaments you and your kid are most likely to find yourselves in. Keep your priorities straight, and you and your family should come out alive. Or better yet, rich.

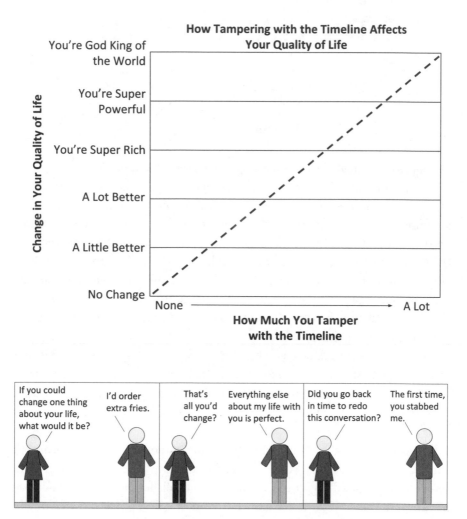

BEFORE LIFE ON EARTH

You take a wrong turn driving to the grocery store and end up back in time before the start of life on earth. Oh, and your kid is still in the back seat. When your GPS says it needs an update, it means it.

Don't panic. Here's what to do.

First, retrace your steps. Maybe you can just drive back through the other way and still have time to pick up milk and eggs before your coupons expire. The grocery list isn't going to finish itself. But let's assume the portal you unknowingly drove through was one-way, and now you're stuck forever. Oh, well. At least you tried.

Next, verify that the earth is actually free of life. The last thing you want is to be surprised by some long-forgotten apex predator. Although if it's early enough, that might just be a slightly more aggressive amoeba. It's hard to be impressed by one of those. Nobody is ever going to make a movie called *Amoeba Park*.

But let's say the planet is truly empty. Earth is past its awkward, molten-lava stage, and has all the prerequisites for life without having life itself—other than the microbes that turn carbon dioxide into oxygen so you can breathe. That means the earth isn't technically devoid of life, but this scenario wouldn't work any other way. I couldn't think of a good reason for you to drive to the grocery store in a space suit.

Focus on the positives. You won't have to worry about paying for your kid's college education. You dodged a bullet there. There also won't be any playdates because there won't be other organisms of any kind, other than those bacteria we're conveniently ignoring. Your weekend schedule will be perpetually clear. I need to find that portal.

On the downside, humans can't photosynthesize their own sunlight, so you'll have to eat something that does. Without plant life, you're sure to starve. But wait: You drove here in the vehicle you use to haul your kid around. Its floor is undoubtedly covered with crushed, expired cereal and pulverized crackers. There should be enough crumbs there to sustain you and your child for the rest of your lives. Since you'll starve when the floor runs out of food, that's literally true. Eat slower.

Since human life will eventually develop independent of you and your child, your main influence will be the records you leave behind. If you want to mess with future archaeologists, leave a message carved in stone. Describe technology that could advance mankind centuries or even millennia. Or maybe just write down some famous literary works from memory and claim credit for yourself. You could be the author of Harry Potter, *The Lord of the Rings*, or even the Bible. Of course, you can probably remember very little of that last one verbatim, and carving words in stone isn't exactly a quick process. Do your best to compress an 800,000-word holy book down to a few sentences. There was God. His son had a rough weekend. Now everybody has to go to church. The end. Add a few adjectives to pad the word count.

You won't need to hunt for food since there won't be any outside your vehicle, so there won't be anything else for you to do. There won't be anything for your kid to do, either. Be prepared to hear them say "I'm bored" all day, every day, for the rest of your life. They'll need to learn to entertain themselves at some point because they'll outlive you. Unless you run out of old Cheerios while you're both still alive, at which point you'll both starve simultaneously. Just make sure your rock-carved stories are protected from the elements so you can reap future literary awards. You might end, but your legacy of poorly executed plagiarism will live on eternally.

Severity of Consequences for Rookie Time Travel Mistakes

Severity of Consequences

| There Is No Future |
| Future Is a Hellscape |
| Future Is a Dystopia |
| Future Is Bleak |
| Future Is a Little Awkward |
| None |

Rookie Mistake:
- Becoming Your Own Grandparent
- Causing Your Parents Not to Exist
- Sneezing and Wiping Out the Roman Empire
- Losing Future Technology Where Hitler Can Find It
- Accidentally Killing the Guy Who Invents Milk Chocolate

THE AGE OF THE DINOSAURS

You watched a YouTube video on how to fix a microwave, so you're pretty sure you can do it yourself—with a little help from your child's tiny hands. They have to be good for something. Thirty seconds later, your kid crosses two wires and both of you are sent back in time to the age of the dinosaurs. Oops.

The dinosaurs ruled the earth for millions of years over several distinct eras, each of which had its own unique climate, flora, and fauna. Nobody cares. If you accidentally get thrown back in time to the age of the dinosaurs, you're fighting a T-rex. If you can beat it, you can defeat any of the lesser dinosaurs that might attack you. The T-rex is nature's perfect killing machine—allegedly. One hundred percent of T-rexes are now dead, so obviously they had a few design flaws.

If you find yourself and your child out in the open facing a T-rex, challenge it to an arm-wrestling contest. There's no scientific literature to suggest T-rexes can understand human language, but there's also none to suggest they can't. Just because T-rexes existed millions of years before humans is no reason to believe one wouldn't pick up the gist of what you're trying to communicate. Flexing your arms is a universal gesture.

If the T-rex accepts your challenge, find a flat rock to use as a table and win several arm-wrestling matches in a row. The T-rex will be so demoralized that it'll slink away, never to bother you or your child again. Or more likely, it will eat you, because T-rexes are notoriously sore losers. You won't know for sure until it's too late.

If the T-rex looks like it might be a spoilsport, have your kid search for weapons. Maybe there's a sharp stick or bazooka lying around. You never know what else has been thrown back in time over the years due to bungled microwave repair. As a parent, you'll have to make a judgment call as to whether or not you're comfortable with your child using a bazooka. But then again, if you challenged a T-rex to an arm-wrestling match, you clearly don't have the best judgment. Let the kid use whatever weapon they want.

If your child can only find a sharpened stick or, worse, a regular stick they have to sharpen themselves, the two of you are in for a hard time. Once the stick is sharpened, instruct your child to sneak up behind the T-rex for a perfunctory stabbing. If the T-rex is still arm-wrestling you at the time, it's a bad idea to do that out loud, since this particular T-rex clearly understands human language. Try to convey the message to your child solely with meaningful facial expressions. Or better yet, discuss this plan with your child in advance. Parents always remember to have the talk about sex but not the one about fighting dinosaurs. Based on your own high school dating record, which one is really more likely?

If you had the dinosaur talk with your kid ahead of time, they'll know what to do. In the middle of your arm-wrestling match, your kid will jump on the T-rex's back and stab it in the head. It's possible your child will penetrate the dinosaur's skull and kill it. It's equally possible the stick will snap in half. Actually, that's way more likely, but you had to try something. Even if your child does penetrate the T-rex's skull, it's unlikely the stick will hit its brain, which is the size of a walnut. It turns out being stupid is a survival advantage. That explains so much.

If you're not confident in your child's brain-stabbing ability (and, really, who is?), tell your kid to move to the side and aim for the T-rex's eye instead. A T-rex with a stick in its eye is somewhat less dangerous than a T-rex without one in its eye. If you have a second child, tell them to simultaneously jab a stick into the other eye so the T-rex will be fully blind. That's why, as a rule, you should always get thrown back in time with at least two kids. Single-child families are a death trap.

Once the T-rex is blind, run away and live your life to the fullest. No other dinosaur will mess with you. It's like beating up the toughest guy on your first day in prison. Force understands force, even when it has a brain too small to be stabbed with a stick.

If eye poking and brain stabbing aren't your thing, you could always hit the earth with an asteroid. I don't know how you would do that. I'm more of a big-idea guy. Or you could stall the T-rex until the next ice age. Better yet, let your kid do the stalling. If they can make you twenty minutes late to leave home every day, surely they can delay a T-rex long enough for the climate to change. Entire glaciers could form in the time it takes them to put on their shoes.

Dinosaur-Like Monsters That Aren't Actually Dinosaurs

Dinosaur-Like Monster	What It Actually Is
Pterodactyl	Giant flappy lizard thing.
Plesiosaur	Scottish tourist trap.
Snapping Turtle	Evil ninja turtle.
That Giant Water Lizard Thing in *Jurassic World*	A giant water lizard thing.
Godzilla	A fun mascot for the nuclear power industry.
Chickens	Dumb birds who left all their dino qualities behind to become delicious.
That Super-Old Relative Who You Can't Stand	The jury is still out.
Barney	The bane of parents everywhere.

ANCIENT ATHENS

One day you click "I agree" on a new app for Crock-Pot recipes, and suddenly you and your child are transported back in time to ancient Athens. Always read the terms and conditions, especially when slow cookers are involved.

Ancient Greece won't be all bad. Sure, there won't be modern medicine, and your life expectancy will be cut in half, but on the bright side, you and your child will both be in the birthplace of democracy. Your kid will see what government looks like when it's truly in the hands of the people, even if those people die from diseases that were easily treatable in your own century. What a time to be briefly alive.

Granted, Athenian democracy wasn't perfect. There were rivalries and intrigue, as there are any time human beings are involved. People are the worst. But for the most part, all Athenians could make their voices heard.

As long as they weren't women. Or foreigners. Or slaves. It turns out people have always been awful to each other. That's another important lesson for your kid to learn.

Have your child watch this small, privileged group of Athenian citizens in action. They voted by dropping a rock in an urn. As you observe them, you'll realize direct democracy works less like a classroom debate and more like an internet forum. Everyone shouts and nobody listens, and those rocks are more likely to be hurled than dropped in a bucket. Democracy hurts.

Use your body to shield your child from the biggest stones. You don't want your kid to be turned off by the electoral process. Sure, it doesn't work much of the time, like when you're being stoned to death, but neither do any of the other systems. Tell your child it's important to make their opinion known, even if they aren't part of the narrowly defined, empowered class at their specific time and place in history. Really, you're just showing your kid that life isn't fair. But they probably guessed that when you were thrown back in time by a Crock-Pot app.

There are other perks to living in ancient Athens. Dressing your child will be much easier, since they can wear a toga every day. The fit is pretty loose, so it'll be hard for your kid to outgrow one. Unfortunately, ancient Greece didn't have washing machines or bleach, and everything they wore was white. Yes, laundry day found a way to get worse.

Be prepared to do everything by hand, unless you get rich enough to have servants. I'm not sure how you could gain wealth in ancient Greece. I guess you could try to profit from modern-day technology, but really, what can you make from scratch? It's not like you can dig up metal and smelt an iPhone. Don't let that stop you from trying, though. You won't have much else to do with your time, besides arguing with strangers and occasionally throwing stones. That was the real secret to Athenian democracy. Voting didn't help anyone on its own, but dodging stones kept everyone fit and spry, greatly enhancing their quality of life. It wasn't so much a system of government as it was a state-sponsored exercise plan.

I'd rather be stoned.

BUBONIC PLAGUE

It's always disappointing when you open your fridge only to find a gaping chasm through space and time that sends you and your child back to medieval Europe during the bubonic plague. You just wanted some eggs.

Now that you're through the fridge portal, there's no going back. But don't fret. Medieval Europe has more to fear from you than you do from it. If your child has been to day care, they've been in contact with enough mutated germs to kill every man, woman, and child who came before you on the timeline. In fact, there's a chance your child, by going back in time, is the one who started the bubonic plague. Don't worry about the time paradox. That's the least confusing part of parenting.

But even though your kid has had practically every disease known to science, they might not have had the specific strain of plague going through Europe at that time. Just to be safe, keep your kid away from anything unsanitary. In medieval Europe, that includes approximately everything. Although the germs back then were not as ferocious as the ones in modern day cares, they were more abundant. When the only waste disposal system is tossing poop out a second-story window, you have to lower your expectations. And carry an umbrella.

To help your child stay plague-free, get a cat, even if your kid has allergies. Light sneezing is better than death by plague. A cat will eat the rats that carry disease-infested fleas. Plus, cats are adorable, and the addiction center in your brain has made them a necessary part of your life. In the absence of cat memes, you'll have to settle for the real thing. What a terrible time to be alive.

As a final precaution, tell your child not to make friends. Being around other people will raise the risk of your kid getting infected by the only disease they haven't had yet. Bacteria aren't Pokémon; your kid doesn't have to catch 'em all. Also, every time one of those new friends dies, you would have to go to their funeral. That's a major time commitment (and more than a little dangerous; see chapter five). Encourage your child to be proactively antisocial to keep your family's schedule free.

If your child does get the plague, all hope isn't lost. Just give your child's immune system a good pep talk. Remind it that your kid spent their early years finding dirty objects on the floor and inserting them into various bodily orifices. The only way to learn a rock doesn't belong up your nose is through trial and error. The bacteria your child is already teeming with should protect their turf against encroaching plague germs. Home-field advantage has to count for something. The competing diseases should kill each other while leaving your child to make a full recovery. That's how medieval medicine works.

Medieval Medical Conditions That Are Now Eradicated

Disease	Symptoms
Butter Churner's Elbow	Detached arm and ruined butter. Everybody is mad at you.
Dungeon Breath	You don't have to tell people you regained your freedom. They can smell it from a mile away.
Lactose Super Tolerance	If you don't drink straight cow's milk, you'll die.
Devil Gut	Burping and light demonic possession.
Siege Stomach	Vomiting after being flung into the air by a catapult.
Pilgrim's Knees	You can't get back up after kneeling at a shrine. Now you have to join the clergy.
Lord Fatigue	The thought of additional fealty literally makes you sick.
Triple Plague	You thought you were done after dying twice. You were wrong.

RENAISSANCE VATICAN

You're saying the Our Father when you flub the last line, instantly banishing you back in time to the Renaissance Vatican along with your kid. Just like your Sunday school teacher warned you.

The Renaissance Catholic Church was at the height of its power, and it used its money to build massive basilicas and other monuments designed and crafted by the great masters. Your child has never been this close to so much valuable, breakable stuff. I recommend a child leash and possibly a muzzle. Your paycheck can't cover rebuilding the Sistine Chapel.

To avoid ruffling any feathers, tell everyone you meet that you're Catholic, even if you're not. The Renaissance popes won't be very welcoming to a Mormon or a Jedi. Before the Protestant Revolution, there were only two options: Catholicism or heresy. Pick a side based on whether you want to visit your preferred afterlife immediately or after a long and fruitful life.

Assuming you avoid getting excommunicated or interrogated to death by an inquisition, you could have a lot of fun at the Vatican. Track down Michelangelo and offer him some painting tips. Maybe he'll paint you on the ceiling as one of those buff, naked men or one of those equally buff, naked women. As for your child, politely request that Michelangelo paint them with their clothes on. If you feel like altering the historical timeline, have your child pose doing some viral teen trend from the present day. I'd list some examples, but they'll already be hopelessly out of date by the printing of this book. The only thing more impressive than teenagers' stupid, dangerous trends is their short attention span. Just make sure whatever viral movement your kid kicks off is more stupid than dangerous. Otherwise your child could accidentally wipe out generations of high schoolers.

Chances are your child will actually spend a lot of time in basilicas and chapels, reverently praying. They'll be asking for a miracle to send them back to the age of Wi-Fi and deep dish pizza. That's understandable. Renaissance Italy didn't have pizza of any thickness, so it wasn't actually Italy's greatest age. If you ask any Italian which they would rather have today, beautiful art that stands the test of time or some cheese on a delicious crust, they'd choose pizza every time. We've seen what Michelangelo could do with a hammer and chisel, but imagine what he could have done with a toaster oven. It truly would have been a golden age, or possibly a golden brown one.

At least the language barrier won't be a problem. No matter which form of Latin or Italian the people around you speak during the Renaissance, you'll be able to communicate with them by gesticulating wildly. Just imagine you're talking to a T-rex. Most of your hand motions will be to ask for forgiveness when your child does something wrong. Shaking your head and shrugging are the universal symbols for "I'm sorry my child got dirty fingerprints all over the high altar." The pope will not be amused, so expect to spend a lot of time cleaning. As Jesus said, "Let the children come to me, but only after they wash their hands."

THE HUNDRED YEARS' WAR

What parent hasn't woken up on a lazy Saturday morning only to discover they've been cast back in time with their child to the Hundred Years' War? It happens to the best of us. And the worst of us, too. That's the great thing about misfortune: It screws us all.

For those of you who haven't had that particular unlucky Saturday morning yet—or who simply didn't pay attention in history class—the Hundred Years' War was a decades-long conflict between France and England for complicated reasons nobody remembers or cares about. The point is, there were two sides, and they didn't like each other very much. It was basically a century-long temper tantrum that depleted the manpower and wealth of two nations and accomplished virtually nothing. So it was just like every war ever.

If you and your child find yourselves in the middle of the Hundred Years' War, figure out who's winning at that time and join their side. Teach your child it's okay to be a bandwagon fan as long as it keeps them alive. Just tell them not to get too attached. You should betray your side the second it's to your advantage. Those are the kind of values that will help your child go far as an employee, a spouse, and a parent. Loyalty and success are usually mutually exclusive.

There are some key indications that it's time to switch sides. If one kingdom has heavily armored knights, and the other has peasants with longbows that can punch through armor like a bullet through tissue paper, it's time to bone up on your old-timey English. Likewise, if the other side just got inspired by a peasant girl who may or may not be hearing voices because she's schizophrenic or eating psychedelic mushrooms, it's time for that vacation to Paris you've been putting off—as long as your child isn't the crazy one. If they are, avoid population centers at all costs. As a general rule, you've failed as a parent if your kid gets burned at the stake.

But hopefully it won't come to that. Stick to the background, try not to fight anybody, and betray your side every chance you get. Don't worry, your treachery will be forgotten. There's a reason history is so boring. Just do what you have to do to keep your kid alive and try not to wake up in the wrong century again. It pays to be a light sleeper.

Wars Almost No One Remembers

War	Why No One Remembers It
Greasers vs. Socs	Nobody in junior high does the required reading.
King Kong vs. Godzilla	All witnesses were eaten.
Great Danish War	No one wants to admit they died over doughnuts.
Vietnam War	High school history classes cut off at the end of World War II.
War on Drugs	Blowing up pot just spreads it to new customers.
War on Poverty	Shooting poor people is seldom popular.
War on War	Pacifists fight dirty.
War on Christmas	The elves are secretly planning their counterattack.

AMERICAN REVOLUTION

It's one of those days: You ran out of milk for your cereal, the cat peed on your shoes, and you and your child were tossed back in time to the American Revolution. Mondays.

On the bright side, this could be a great history lesson for your kid. I mean the revolution, not the cat pee or the lack of milk. Who needs calcium when you could start your day with a hearty dose of patriotism? On the darker side, this particular time travel trip could also be a chance for you to single-handedly lose the American Revolution and turn the world's only remaining superpower into a perpetual colony of Great Britain. Tread lightly. Actually, don't do that. Recklessly barge in and change whatever you want like a real American.

Take your child to see every battle, and use your knowledge of history to "predict" who will win. You'll have to use your outdoor voice because wars are loud. Your child will be in awe of your feigned military brilliance, and word of your exploits will spread. Soon, George Washington will want to meet you. Hopefully by then your shoes will no longer smell like cat pee.

Tell Washington everything you can about history to sway the military campaign in his favor. Washington will win the war so decisively that the colonies will invade the United Kingdom. Then the UK will be a US colony. To pay for the cost of the war, the US will tax its UK subjects without representation, causing a new Revolutionary War, but in reverse. I'm not sure how this helps you or your child, but just go along with it. When in doubt, dump more tea in the harbor.

While doing all of this, impress upon your child several important lessons. First, never wear a red coat in battle. Not for any tactical reasons. It just looks tacky. Bad fashion killed more British than bullets ever did. Second, don't go to Valley Forge in the winter. There are better vacation destinations. That place earned all those one-star reviews. Finally, never underestimate the tenacity of a scrappy underdog, especially if that underdog is aided by an unscrupulous time traveler who isn't afraid to change world history to help their own country. USA! USA!

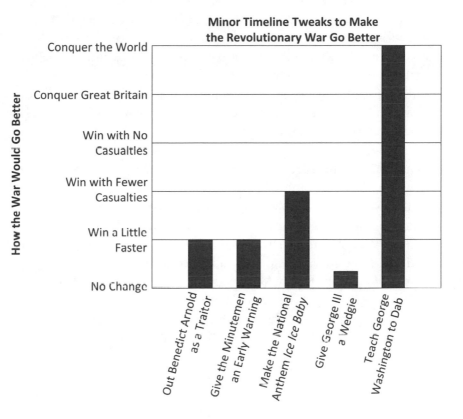

AMERICA IN THE 1950S

Your kid turns on an old TV in an antique store. It sparks once, then sends you and your kid back in time to the 1950s. The sign said "Don't touch" for a reason.

Being a parent in the 1950s will be very different from being a parent today. Rather than worrying that your kid's school will be shot up by a social deviant, you'll worry about it being blown up by a nuclear strike. Ah, the good old days. At least there was a foolproof defense back then. In the event of a nuclear attack, kids would duck and cover under their assigned seats. Everyone knows that after the atomic blasts at Hiroshima and Nagasaki, the only things left standing were elementary school desks.

The constant threat of nuclear annihilation aside, being a parent in the 1950s will be easier than being a parent today. No one will look at you askew if you let your child roam the neighborhood like a feral cat. When the street-lights come on, your kid will either come home or they won't. Parents back then had a much greater respect for natural selection. It was an era when car seats were a fringe curiosity and parachutes were for cowards. Real men broke the fall with their faces and then walked it off. You won't have to worry about your kid hurting themselves in the 1950s. They will get hurt. You just won't be worried about it. Children back then walked around with broken glass and rusty metal embedded in them at all times because they didn't know life any other way. If you don't have at least a little tetanus, are you even alive?

Of course, there will be some dangers you have to watch out for. You won't have to worry about internet bullies, but your kid might be waylaid by a rogue sock hop. Tell your child to back away if anyone asks them to take their shoes off. Your child also might be accused of being a communist. This is obviously absurd since your child has never believed in sharing anything, but logic has no place in the Red Scare. If you want to know how to survive that, see chapter nine on witch hunts. And tell your kid to listen to rock and roll, which everyone knows burns communists like fire.

LATE-STAGE SUN

You're making brownies with your kid when you forget your mom's recipe, so you add three teaspoons of this and two tablespoons of that. Then—poof—you and your kid are teleported billions of years into the future to right before the sun swallows the earth. I guess it was supposed to be one tablespoon.

When the sun expands to swallow the earth, it will take up most of the sky and make the planet blisteringly hot. By that point, all other humans will have died—but probably not from the sun. Seriously, we do so many stupid things, there's no way we'll live long enough for the heat to kill us. More likely, we'll have killed ourselves with nuclear weapons or an engineered super-virus or chain emails that promise bad luck if we don't forward them. If only we had hit "send."

So how are you and your child supposed to make it on a scorched, barren planet with almost no other life? First, apply sunscreen. Hopefully you were holding a bottle of it while making brownies. A giant fusion reaction is no match for SPF 50. Slather the sunscreen on your child every hour, and don't let them go swimming. The water would wash off the sunscreen, and also it's literally boiling. On the plus side, lobsters will cook themselves.

Even after applying sunscreen, keep your child in the shade. This shouldn't be hard since it will be too hot for your kid to move. You won't feel like doing much, either. If you want, you can work on your tan. Without sunscreen, it'll take about two seconds to go from pale to on fire. The solar apocalypse will be a real time saver.

TIMED OUT

Parenting is the same in every age. No matter when or where you go, your child will constantly be in mortal peril, and you'll be exhausted from saving them. The biggest difference will be your audience. In some eras, you'll be closely scrutinized by other parents. In others, there won't be anyone else alive to watch you. Don't think that will spare you from rebuke. You'll always travel with your harshest critic: yourself.

In a way, we're all time travelers. Normally, we just go in one direction at the rate of one day every twenty-four hours. But even if you find some convoluted reason to travel backward or forward in time, your crushing responsibility to keep your child safe will stay the same. Parental angst is timeless.

To make sure you keep yourself and your child safe as you travel through time, keep these dos and don'ts in mind:

✓ **Do** carry a travel bag at all times since you could be tossed into any other time at any time.

✗ **Don't** be intimidated. Trust your ability to be a mediocre parent in any era.

✓ **Do** tell your child what happened. When you can't get Wi-Fi because you're in the Renaissance, it's best to remind your child it's not your fault.

✘ **Don't** tell your kid it actually is your fault. You should have taken basic precautions against accidental time travel, like putting up a safety railing.

✓ **Do** keep your phone charged. You won't be able to call anyone if you get sent back to the Middle Ages, but at least you can play a few hours of *Bejeweled*.

✘ **Don't** brush up on history. If you ever make it back to the present time, you'll be the one writing the textbook. History will be whatever you say it is.

✓ **Do** take time to admire the marvels of your new time period. Unless it's a time before air-conditioning and flushing toilets. Then you're trapped in an ancient hellscape that you should try to escape right away.

✘ **Don't** worry about the timeline. If you have to disrupt the entire course of human events to appease a temper tantrum, so be it.

Time travel is no harder or easier than any other challenge you'll face as a parent. Keep these tips in mind, and prepare for the worst in any age. You'll never be disappointed.

CHAPTER 8

SCI-FI SITUATIONS

What if the future is awful? Welcome to the plot of every science fiction movie ever. You don't have to travel to the future to see just how bad it will be. Popular sci-fi books and films give us a preview today. This chapter will discuss how to protect your kid from the specific dangers that exist solely in the realm of science fiction—for now. A hypothetical dystopian future can become the real dystopian present in the blink of an eye. To protect us all, don't blink. I'll send eye drops.

ALIEN ABDUCTION

So your kid was abducted by aliens.

Don't beat yourself up. It's not like books and movies have been warning you about this exact danger since at least the 1950s. Oh, wait.

At least it's not too late to get your kid back. First, ask yourself how badly you want to save your child. It better be really, really badly. If your commitment is anything less than total, you won't have what it takes for this rescue mission: a total lifestyle change, some clever deceit, and some light probing. If that's not for you, it's best to write off this whole parenting experiment and just get a cat. They almost never get abducted by aliens.

But if you're still all-in on getting your kid back, continue to step two: Get yourself abducted. This is harder than it sounds. Everyone knows aliens only prey on isolated rednecks. If you want to be abducted, you'll have to become one, too. This isn't something you can fake. Advanced alien races can use their technology to tell a real redneck from a poser. When you say "y'all," you better mean it.

If you want to be a real redneck, you can't be subtle. To be the aliens' first choice (well, technically second choice after your kid) out of seven billion people, you'll have to be the biggest redneck ever. Find a house in the country with no running water or electricity. Then listen to nothing but country music. This will be a challenge without electricity, so you'll have to play it yourself as a one-person band. Make sure that band features a jug, a banjo, and two cases of light beer. And yes, light beer is an instrument. Ask anyone at karaoke night.

Next, encourage your dog to run off with your pickup truck and your spouse. You might have to take the preliminary steps of getting a pickup and a spouse. If you're afraid of a little prep work, this mission isn't for you. To speed up your rescue attempt, become a redneck months or years before your kid is abducted. It's never too early to be a hillbilly.

Once you succeed at getting abducted, move on to the third step: probing. This is where you'll turn the tables. No one knows why aliens probe people. If they have the technology to travel faster than light, you'd think they'd have developed a basic CT scan. Maybe probing is their kink. Whatever. I'd rather not know.

When the aliens probe you, make sure what they find is so disruptive they abandon abductions altogether. There's only one logical choice: glitter. Coat your food with it in the weeks leading up to your abduction. Once the aliens probe you, the glitter will get everywhere, and they'll never, ever get rid of it. Disintegrating you would only spread the glitter further since those reflective particles can neither be created nor destroyed. They existed before the dawn of time, and they'll be here long after the universe ends. Unwilling to trifle with a walking glitter bomb, the aliens will be forced to let you go. And all your freedom cost you was the curse of twinkling for the rest of your life. It's almost worth it.

When the aliens try to kick you off their ship, refuse to go unless they also send your child with you. Otherwise, you'll stay onboard and spread the sparkly plague to every corner of the ship. As an intelligent race, the aliens will immediately cave in to your demands and return you and your child to earth. You'll be safe, but the benefits of your heroism will pretty much end there. You'll have done a great service for mankind, but no one will ever believe you except for your fellow rednecks and a few daytime talk shows. Charge for every TV appearance to exploit your minor celebrity for maximum profit. Your family has to eat, even if your spouse never did come back with your dog.

But even once you escape, the whole episode will leave you with one lingering question: If aliens only abduct rednecks, why did your child get abducted in the first place? I have some bad news: Your kid was a closet redneck all along. They probably never told you because of your anti-redneck bigotry. Or maybe they were in denial themselves. Either way, after your involuntary space adventure is over, you and your kid will need to have a heart-to-heart talk. At that point, you'll have three options: You could stay a redneck yourself so you and your child have something in common; you could go back to being a non-redneck but accept your redneck child for who they really are; or you could disown your redneck child because country music has the same effect on you as waterboarding. Only you can decide which approach is right for your family. Hint: It's not option three.

CYLONS

In the *Battlestar Galactica* reboot, Cylons are robots disguised as people who want to annihilate the human race. This makes complete sense. Cylons hate us because they look like us. They imitated us completely, right down to our self-loathing.

Dealing with Cylons will be hard for parents. When anyone could be a homicidal robot hell-bent on destroying mankind, it's tough to find a trustworthy babysitter.

To verify whether or not the person you're dealing with is a Cylon, have your child play in front of them. Really let your kid go nuts. The more running, yelling, and screaming, the better. Don't step in to restrain your kid in any way. If the other person instantly parent-shames you, they're a human—and also a jerk. If they just stand there without getting annoyed, they're a Cylon. Only a robot has that kind of self-control.

Another test is to see if there are any exact duplicates of the person you're dealing with. When you see a potential babysitter's picture, check if that picture has been used anywhere else on the internet. If it turns out someone else under another name looks exactly like them, they're a Cylon. Or a catfish. Both are dangerous.

Continue your search until you find someone who looks unique. The uglier, the better. Cylons are almost always good-looking. Even robots are too vain to let their appearance go. If you spot someone who looks like the Hunchback of Notre Dame, you've found your next babysitter. Unless they charge too much. Then just stay home and watch your own kids—as long as you're not a Cylon yourself.

THE DEATH STAR

Not everyone has the luxury of reliable child care while battling the Empire. Sure, the most famous rebel pilots in the Star Wars universe rush off to fight evil child-free. But what if your babysitter cancels on the day you're scheduled to blow up the Death Star? Don't worry, you can be the mother or father you've always wanted to be and also destroy a moon-sized super-weapon. You really can have it all.

Before you take your child with you on this dangerous mission, make sure you've exhausted all child care alternatives. Is there seriously no one else on Yavin 4 who can watch your kid for, like, thirty minutes? I mean, all the people running around those glowing screens seem occupied, but I'm sure you can find someone who's only pretending to be busy. Every organization has a person like that. It's usually me.

If you can't find a human babysitter, consider whether or not you're comfortable with C-3PO watching your child. He did nothing of value to destroy the Death Star. He just stood around and annoyed people. Would you trust him to keep your child alive for a short period of time while you save everyone's lives? I wouldn't. C-3PO is too stiff. I don't think he could bend down to pick up a kid. In fact, it would be easy for children to topple him like a snowspeeder circling an AT-AT. How would he get up? He never displays that level of agility in any of the movies. If your child is mobile enough to walk, C-3PO would be outmatched. Even if your kid isn't mobile yet, you still shouldn't leave your child with him. Those shiny metal hands would be terrible at changing diapers.

With C-3PO ruled out, the only option left is to take your child into battle with you. If you're a Y-wing pilot, this isn't a deal-breaker. The backward-facing gunner position could more than accommodate a car seat. Of course, that would mean you'd have to leave your normal gunner back at base. Is your child old enough to operate the rear cannons? Now is a good time to find out. Set your kid back there and tell them not to shoot any friendlies. Then watch as your kid accidentally takes out half your own force. On second thought, turn off the cannon controls and just go without a gunner for this mission. That's why Y-wings took 100 percent casualties in the first Death Star attack.

If you're in an X-wing, however, there's no second seat. There is room for an astromech droid, but that slot is exposed to the vacuum of space. You can't tell R2-D2 to stay home while your kid rides with their head hanging out of the X-wing. Besides, astromech droids navigate, and you can't trust your child with that duty. If you hand your child a map of space, you'd start out heading for the Death Star and end up at a burger joint. That's great if you want French fries but less than ideal if you want to cast off the yoke of Imperial oppression. Get that order to go.

That means that, realistically, your child will have to sit on your lap for the Death Star trench run. If your child is small, that won't be a big deal. If they're a teenager, maybe don't bring them at all. They can probably look after themselves for a few minutes. That's a lie. But how much damage can they really cause when compared with the imminent destruction of Yavin 4 by the Death Star's superlaser? Probably as much, if not more. Just wait until your kid gets their hands on your car keys. Either way, you don't have much choice. Tell your teenager to sit tight at the base and that you'll be back in half an hour or less. Expect them to throw between one and three parties in that time. "Sith" is just another word for teenager.

If you're bringing a baby with you, take them out of their car seat and strap them into your five-point crash harness with you. Your weight will push against them every time you make a turn, but there's simply no room for a baby carrier in those confined quarters. You could let them float freely through the cabin instead, but they would bounce around quite a bit as you dodge TIE fighters. I recommend strapping your baby in and hoping for the best. Or at least hoping they use their freakishly strong baby grip to hold on really tight.

If your child is old enough to understand instructions, tell them to be as quiet as possible so you can listen for any last-minute Force advice from Obi-Wan Kenobi. You don't want to miss his message from beyond the grave because your kid is angrily demanding that you roll down the window in the middle of space. Don't roll down the window in the middle of space.

To make things easier, ask any dead Jedi you know to contact you before you have your child in the X-wing. The Force doesn't really work that way, so you probably won't have a good contact number. Just say it out loud to no one in particular. With luck, the dead Jedi in question will give you the advice you need. Or not. Obi-Wan was never great at dealing with challenging family situations.

As for firing the torpedo down the Death Star's exhaust shaft, I recommend not using the Force. The Force is based on emotions, and the main emotion you'll be feeling is anger as your child frustrates you at every turn. You'll blow up the Death Star, but only by giving in to the dark side. If you actually want the good guys to win, relax a little and shoot as best you can on your own. Or better yet, hand the torpedo controls over to your child. Kids are experts at causing improbable amounts of destruction. If they take the final shot, they're guaranteed to blow up the Death Star. Don't worry. There are more Death Stars where that came from.

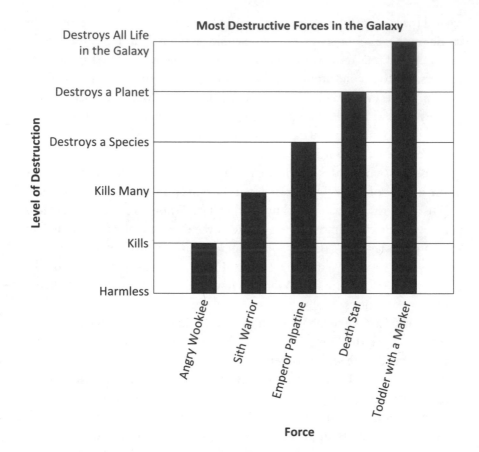

Most Destructive Forces in the Galaxy

Level of Destruction (y-axis, bottom to top): Harmless, Kills, Kills Many, Destroys a Species, Destroys a Planet, Destroys All Life in the Galaxy

Force (x-axis): Angry Wookiee, Sith Warrior, Emperor Palpatine, Death Star, Toddler with a Marker

Worst Parental Figures in Star Wars

Parental Figure	Why They Were Terrible
Rey's Parents	Traded their daughter for drinking money.
Uncle Owen	Didn't support Luke's dreams. Didn't avoid getting incinerated by stormtroopers. All-around disappointment.

Aunt Beru	Always ready with a refreshing glass of blue milk for Luke. Never asked if he was lactose intolerant.
Padmé	Died of a broken heart over the worst husband ever, even though her newborn twins needed her. Not exactly mother of the year.
General Leia	Had a kid with a scruffy-looking nerf herder.
Han Solo	Trusted a weird uncle to train his son.
Darth Vader	Wanted his son to join him, but cut off his hand instead. Not the best bonding experience.
The Force	Fathered Anakin. Never paid child support.

DOCTOR WHO

It's always alarming when a human-like alien appears out of nowhere to whisk your kid away across time and space in a spaceship disguised as a police box. "It's bigger on the inside," the alien will say, as if it's the box's size and not the kidnapping that bothers you. But at least the bigger-on-the-inside thing is true. Nobody wants their kid to roam the universe in a box the size of a Porta-Potty.

The owner of that box is the Doctor, and if they want to take your kid, you won't have much say in the matter. You won't even have time to try. Since the Doctor can travel through time, they could bring your child back at the exact moment they left, even if the adventure in between took hours, days, or an entire lifetime. To reduce the awkwardness of this situation, insist on accompanying your child on all time travel adventures. This will be better than the misadventures described in the time travel chapter because in this case you'll be going on purpose and with someone who knows what they're doing. Sort of.

In practice, while traveling with the Doctor, you'll have to be the adult in every situation. The Doctor might keep you safe, but they also might accidentally abandon you to die because they get distracted by one of the many potentially universe-ending events that seem to crop up at least once an episode. It will be up to you to keep a close eye on your child to make sure they don't get disintegrated in the process. And, no, you can't just go back in time to save your child's life. That's forbidden for completely arbitrary reasons that change by the episode. Life isn't fair. Science fiction isn't, either.

The good news is that, as a parent, you'll be especially well suited to deal with certain enemies, like the Weeping Angels, evil statues that can only move when no one is looking. If they touch you, they send you back in time and drain the energy from the life you would have lived. You absolutely shouldn't let a Weeping Angel drain your life force. That's what children are for. But it won't come to that. As you already know from the section on tigers, all parents have eyes in the back of their heads. If you're around, Weeping Angels will be permanently frozen in place. If the Doctor brought parents along on every adventure, the Weeping Angels wouldn't have been a problem in the first place. Maybe that's why the Doctor prefers to hang out with kids or young adults unencumbered by offspring. Life isn't an adventure without completely avoidable danger.

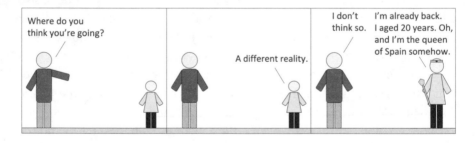

E.T.

Are you worried your child is secretly harboring a small, friendly alien in your house? You should be. Aliens, even seemingly harmless ones like in the movie *E.T.*, are strangers, and your child shouldn't talk to them without your express permission. If your child starts acting secretive, investigate immediately. Maybe it won't be because of an alien. You could get lucky and discover your kid is just on drugs.

One of the first warning signs of alien cohabitation is candy. Friendly aliens can be lured out of hiding with small pieces of it placed on the ground. Presumably that's why the alien crossed the galaxy in the first place. They've mastered interstellar travel, but they don't know how to wrap chocolate in a hard candy shell. If you see your child place a trail of candy on the floor, ground them on the spot. Even if the trail doesn't draw out an alien, it's sure to attract ants. Then, when your kid is out of the room, brush any dirt off the candy and eat it yourself. After all the germs your kid has exposed you to, your immune system can take it.

If you don't stop the friendly alien infestation before it starts, there will be dire consequences. An alien like E.T. will want to use your phone. One time I made a twenty-minute call to Germany and it cost me fifty-four dollars. Imagine what it would cost to call another solar system. That alien will bankrupt your family for generations to come.

Friendly aliens also attract government agents. The last thing you want is for your entire house to be covered in plastic as the FBI investigates. What will the neighbors think? Probably that you have a bug infestation, which is almost as embarrassing. At least the agents won't be armed. I mean, they will be, but somebody will edit out their guns and give them walkie-talkies after the fact. Thank goodness you'll be safe retroactively.

GREMLINS

What happens if you and your family encounter gremlins like the ones from the classic '80s movie? Most people don't realize that movie was a documentary, mainly because it wasn't. But I refuse to believe it was entirely fictional. Gremlins haunted my nightmares for years, and now it's time for me to get even. Here's how to save your family from the bane of my childhood.

Gremlin encounters are unavoidable. At some point, your kid will bring home a mogwai. Those are the cute little fur balls that turn into gremlins if you feed them after midnight. They operate under the same basic rules as toddlers: They're too cute for you to get rid of, but they're never more than a snack away from turning into monsters.

Unlike mogwai, which are basically Furbies that poop, gremlins aren't cute at all. They're green, scaly, toddler-sized monsters with a fondness for mischief and homicide, though not necessarily in that order. Unlike toddlers, which have no known weaknesses, gremlins have a number of vulnerabilities. The most obvious of these is sunlight, which burns them alive. Considering that there's a giant ball of fire in the sky that pummels the earth with a never-ending cascade of solar rays, that's a bit of a problem for all of gremlin-kind. Seriously, the sun hasn't taken a day off in almost five billion years. It's definitely cosmic employee of the month.

So when your part of the earth is facing the sun—a time period known colloquially as "daytime" or "The Sunning"—you're in the clear. Just walk outside and any gremlins that follow you will melt. Of course, the sun also poses a danger to your toddler, which is why you have to slather them in sunscreen. Now that I think about it, toddlers might actually be gremlins. Get a DNA test just in case.

Unfortunately, the earth keeps on turning, and for part of every twenty-four-hour rotation, your home will face away from the sun. This period is known as "nighttime" or "The Time of Stalling" if you have a small child who doesn't want to go to bed. Without death rays shooting down from the sky, how are you supposed to kill the gremlins? By being the kind of parent you were always meant to be.

Gremlins don't have superpowers, so they're as vulnerable to physical threats as your own child. Everything kills them. Knives. Microwaves. You. Basically all the stuff you go out of your way to protect your child from every single day. To kill gremlins, un-childproof your house. Take off the child locks. Remove the safety covers from electrical outlets. Leave the good scissors where little hands can reach them. With all these dangers exposed, the gremlins should be dead within minutes. Seriously, your house is a death trap. Just ask any super-parent on the internet.

GODZILLA

Nothing disrupts your child's closely regulated schedule like a Godzilla attack. It doesn't matter how good a parent you are. Once a 350-foot-tall monster destroys the city, nap time is pretty much over.

When Godzilla starts a rampage, calmly move your child away from the destruction zone and head out to the countryside. Godzilla is mainly concerned with demolishing tall buildings. That's why there's no footage of him pointlessly stomping empty farm fields. If you already live in a rural area, congratulations: Nothing in your life is worth destroying. Sit back and watch as those condescending city-dwellers get their comeuppance. Not that it will bother them. Like crime and traffic, radioactive monsters are just a part of city life.

If escape isn't an option, remember that you've dealt with Godzilla's kind before. He's basically a giant toddler. He only destroys cities because he wants attention. He's not even hungry, which is why he never eats anything he crushes. Not that skyscrapers have any nutritional value anyway. They're mostly fiber.

Deal with this supersized temper tantrum the same way you deal with the tiny human kind: Ignore it. This will infuriate Godzilla. He'll stomp his feet and blow his radioactive fire even harder. But after a while, he'll tire himself out. Just make sure you don't flinch, even if his feet slam down an inch from your face. And if they land on top of you, well, at least you'll die with the moral high ground, even as you're literally stomped into it.

Once Godzilla calms down, you can show him the error of his ways, presuming you avoided being flattened. Tell him to go stand in the corner and think about what he's done. There aren't any corners big enough to fit Godzilla, so he'll have to go back to the ocean. The Marianas Trench sounds like a good place to cool off. Of course, those techniques seldom work with a human toddler, so the odds of them working with a giant monster are slim to none. Still, you have to make the attempt. Parenting is all about futilely doing the right thing so you can shrug and say at least you tried. If you die giving Godzilla a stern lecture, you'll be remembered as a martyr for doing the right thing. Or you could just stick to the original plan and run away in terror with your kid. That's what I'd do.

Deadliest Giant Monsters

Monster	What Makes Them Deadly
King Kong	Endangers the world's banana supply.
Graboids from the movie *Tremors*	Have a taste for Kevin Bacon.
Sandworms	Don't want the spice to flow.
Sarlacc	Never moves but still gets fed. The most efficient hunter in the galaxy.
Mothra	Harasses lighthouses.

Rodan	Cuts through commercial airspace without filing a flight plan.
Modern Godzilla	Like the classic Godzilla, but on CrossFit.
Your Own Insecurities	Wow, they're big.

THE MATRIX

Your bizarre daily experiences as a parent already make you question whether any of this is real. It turns out it's not. The entire world is a computer simulation designed to distract humans as machines use our comatose bodies like batteries. The upside is there are literally no consequences for your actions in the computer world as long as you don't anger the machine overlords. Think electric thoughts and you'll go far. Your mind will, anyway. Your body will stay in one place for your entire life until you're totally drained. That's parenting in a nutshell.

As a parent, you're the most likely person to see through the Matrix. When your child throws a twenty-minute fit because you cut up their grapes, you'll realize none of this could happen in a rational universe. Unfortunately, your child might also recognize the unreality of the Matrix. If that happens, they'll suddenly have unlimited energy within the confines of the machine. If you think your kid is hard to deal with now, wait until they enter God mode. Your child was impossible long before they became unstoppable.

As a parent, you'll have to decide if you want to live in a fake world that gives you everything you could possibly want or a real one that's harsh and unforgiving but offers an actual future. Your child, of course, will choose the computer world. It's the ultimate triumph of screen time over reality. Why would your kid want to overthrow the machines when the machines have basically given them unlimited access to the perfect virtual reality game? As long as you personally realize it isn't real, you can zoom around like a superhero, lording your powers over the unfortunate masses who lack your self-awareness. Then again, the machines might notice and put the kibosh on your child's fun, and that's when it'll be time to fight back. All great revolutions start when a hero is slightly inconvenienced by an authority figure. It's the Stamp Act all over again.

Just don't expect life to be any better if you and your kid escape the Matrix. In the real, post-apocalyptic world, everyone eats a goopy oatmeal-like paste instead of your child's favorite brand of cereal. At that point, the machines will be the least of your problems. You'll spend most of your time battling your own child in a vain attempt to stop them from voluntarily starving to death. You'll be tempted to go back into the machine just to get them some macaroni and cheese. Don't give in. Once the revolution starts, the machines will take away your superpowers in the Matrix. Then the computer world will be exactly as lame as the real one. Talk about a hard truth. The ultimate dystopia is just your normal life.

If you do manage to defeat the machines in the real world and destroy the Matrix, you'll be filled with regret. Seriously, what does it matter if your entire life is just one long, super-vivid dream? For all we know, the "real" world is also a secondary Matrix in some larger universe. We might be stuck in a never-ending series of Matrices, with each Matrix's machines exploited by smarter, more powerful machines one Matrix higher. Your odds of survival are best if you stay in the Matrix you started in. There's no sense in breaking through to new realities full of increasingly more powerful enemies. Plus staying put is easier. The best reality is the one that requires you to do the least.

THE STAR TREK UNIVERSE

If you find yourself living in the United Federation of Planets four hundred years in the future, congratulations. You reside in a utopia free from hunger, disease, and war. But as every single Star Trek episode proves, paradise can be deceiving. In the Star Trek universe, there's no money because replicators can create anything you want for free, yet there are still enough problems to fill a weekly hour-long time slot. And that's the world where you'll be raising a child. Set phasers to stun.

The hardest part of raising a kid in the Star Trek universe won't be secretive alien cabals or Federation politics. The biggest challenge will simply be the lack of mindless entertainment. Apparently the future is so perfect that no one needs TV. At night when they're off duty, crew members go back to their quarters and stare at the walls. If they're feeling ambitious, they might ask the computer to play some music. Endless boredom feels better with a soundtrack.

Now take that same futuristic boredom chamber and add a kid. Your next-door neighbors on the *Enterprise* will love that. Kids innately sense when they need to be quiet, and do the opposite. That's why they go ballistic on planes. There's no escape and nothing you can do to calm them down. Traveling on the *Enterprise* is essentially a seven-year flight with no cartoons. Pray the rest of the crew doesn't throw your family out the airlock.

In place of TV, many ships in the Star Trek universe have a holodeck. It's basically a perfectly immersive 3D video game that tries to kill you. It

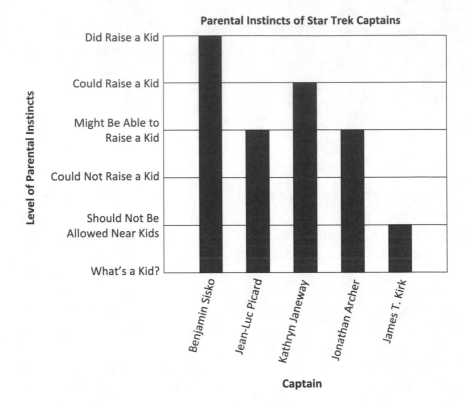

Parental Instincts of Star Trek Captains

wasn't designed to be a futuristic murder machine, but that's how it works out every time someone turns it on. There's always a glitch, and suddenly the damage buffer is turned off and you can really die. If an Xbox or PlayStation game really killed kids, there would be a public outcry. But the Star Trek holodecks try to kill people every other episode and everyone seems okay with that. Illogical indeed.

The best solution is to take advantage of a classic Star Trek trope: time travel. The first time you get thrown back in time, alter history so that TV never falls out of favor. Maybe that means humans will never reach the stars or eliminate war, disease, and famine. But if you can make TV stick around, your kid will have a safe distraction, and that will make your life easier. And in the end, that's more important than one more failed utopia. Your own perfect world is just thirty minutes of peace.

AN X-FILES INVESTIGATION

If you and your child find yourselves caught up in an X-Files investigation, watch your step. The last thing you want is for some pushy government operative to lock up your kid under suspicion of being a cryptid or a ghost child or a secret evil twin. It's an easy mistake to make. Your kid is weird twenty-four hours a day. There's no way all those unusual sounds they make are human. Tell your kid to act normal for once. Actually, don't, or they'll be self-conscious and act weirder than usual. Instead, tell your kid nothing and let them get curious and ask a million questions. Hopefully that will annoy the FBI agents enough that they leave you both alone.

If the FBI interviews you as a witness to a paranormal event, immediately volunteer all the information you have. Nothing drags out an investigation or a slow-moving episode more than random townsfolk who hide information for no reason. "Well, yeah, I have clear, high-definition video of the monster you're looking for, but I didn't show you before because I didn't want you to think I was crazy." When an unexplained force is murdering people, maybe keeping up appearances shouldn't be your top priority. Just a thought.

Tell your child to be equally forthcoming. This will be a challenge for them since they're used to keeping even the most mundane details of their life a secret. Maybe they did multiplication tables at school; maybe they made pagan sacrifices to the occult. Based on the indifferent shrug they gave you, you'll never know.

No matter what you tell your kid to do, expect them to give the FBI the wrong information. For young children, the past, present, future, and their imagination are all one and the same. If you ask my preschooler if she's ever seen an alien, she'll say "yes." If you ask her if she's never seen an alien, she'll also say "yes." And if you ask her if all she can say is "yes," she'll say "no," and then "yes." And then she'll steal your French fries.

THE FUTURE IS NOW

As a parent, you'll never be caught off guard when the seemingly perfect world of tomorrow turns into the futuristic hellscape of today. You're raising a kid. Been there, done that.

With your extensive experience in unpleasant surprises, plus the wisdom from this chapter, you should be more than prepared to guide your child through any sci-fi nightmare. As you do, keep these dos and don'ts in mind:

✘   **Don't** assume that as technology gets better, life gets better. A sci-fi novel is just seventy thousand words of pessimism. You should feel right at home.

✓   **Do** take time to admire the marvels of the sci-fi world. Even the worst post-apocalyptic nightmare has a nice hotel or two.

- ✘ **Don't** assume technology equals intelligence. People in the future will be just as dumb as people today, but with smarter apps to order takeout.

- ✔ **Do** be consistent about discipline, no matter how tough times get. You can't let your kid out of time-out just because there's a Borg invasion.

- ✘ **Don't** shun alternate ways of doing things just because they're new. Making teenagers battle to the death for food for their district isn't that much worse than putting another week of groceries on your maxed-out Visa.

- ✔ **Do** try to make the world a better place, but only for yourself and your child. It's okay to make everyone else's lives in this dystopian nightmare a little worse.

- ✘ **Don't** get discouraged. If you can survive a teething baby, you can survive in a reality where baby aliens burst out of people's chests. Always wear a protective sweater vest.

With the help of this list, you can protect your child just as well in a potential future as you can in the real present. Which is to say, not very well at all.

CHAPTER 9

CLASSICAL LITERATURE

Literary plots that could really kill your child aren't limited to the alternate realities of science fiction. The dangers mentioned in classical books are timeless. But could the imaginings of a long-dead author really be a threat to your child? Does Holden Caulfield think people are phony?

Life imitates art. Then people write books about those real events, and art imitates life in a self-sustaining cycle of danger that's out to get your kid. It's possible each of the following dangers from classical literature will become real at some point in the future or has already been real at some point in the past. Or maybe you and your child will literally be sucked into a book. Crazier things have happened. But mostly just in books.

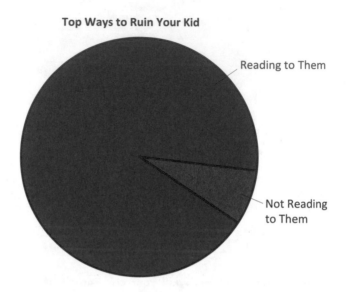

Top Ways to Ruin Your Kid

Reading to Them

Not Reading to Them

CHARLIE AND THE CHOCOLATE FACTORY

Never in the history of capitalism has there been a facility more dangerous than Willy Wonka's chocolate factory. The tour group had a shockingly low survival rate. No wonder Wonka kept the place sealed off from the public for so long. Those deaths weren't accidental, either. He knew excited, sugared-up kids would never follow the rules, and he knew the consequence for breaking those rules was death by candy, yet he did the tour anyway to teach any survivors a lesson. If you murder a bunch of kids on a factory tour so they'll learn about morality, you're not a businessman; you're a serial killer in a top hat.

And, yes, I know the kids technically "survived." But really, every candy trap should have been fatal. Unlike the book and movie, I won't gloss over serious hazards to appease a young audience. In real life, those kids on the tour would have been gone forever. Sure, the parents would keep knocking on Wonka's door, asking where their kids went, but he'd never tell them.

And his lawyers are better than their lawyers, so he'd never be charged with anything. He might get his Oompa-Loompas from Loompaland, but his attorneys come straight from hell.

Besides, the community can't afford to lose Wonka. He has the only factory in town. If he went to jail, his Oompa-Loompas would run amok. They had no qualms about setting deadly candy traps for children, so just imagine what they'd do when cut loose with nothing to lose. The only thing worse than their sweet tooth is their lust for blood.

That's why, if your child finds a golden ticket, you should tear it up so your kid is never in harm's way in the first place. Scratch that—a golden ticket is worth a lot of money. Sell it on the dark web to the highest bidder and then pretend you never saw it. Be sure to wipe off all your fingerprints first.

If you do get roped into going on the tour, take every possible precaution. Inside the chocolate factory, tell your kid not to touch anything. This won't work because your kid is in a chocolate factory. There's no place else on earth where your kid will have a greater incentive to touch stuff. Your child will poke, lick, or chomp everything in sight, including the stuff that's not made of candy. Watch your fingers.

At least tell your kid not to lie to Wonka. Don't tell Wonka the truth, either. Say nothing. If he asks you or your child something, stare blankly into space, giving no sign that you even heard the question. With luck, Wonka will assume you and your kid are both deaf and mute and thus not a threat. Your goal isn't to have your child inherit the candy murder factory. You simply want them to survive—and maybe sell the movie rights to the story. A kid can dream.

Deadliest Types of Candy

Candy	How It's Deadly
Nerds	Anger actual nerds, who kill you with science.
Peanut M&Ms	Today peanuts are considered slightly more deadly than ricin.
Warheads	Inure kids to nuclear weapons.
Reese's Pieces	Choking hazards.
Candy Necklace	Strangling hazard.
Candy Cane	Stabbing hazard.
Jawbreakers	Breaks jaws.
Gobstoppers	Stops gobs.

FAHRENHEIT 451

If the world suddenly imitates *Fahrenheit 451*, you're in luck. The entire premise is that books are banned. For the rest of society, it's a disaster. But for the parent of a young child, it's a dream come true.

Think about what it's actually like to read a book to your kid. The first time you read a story, you're excited to share one of your favorite tales from your own childhood. But then your kid wants to hear it every night. Then six times a night. Then sixty. That's when you learn what children's books are really like. *The Cat in the Hat* is somewhere between seventy-five and a thousand pages long depending on how tired you are when you open it. Spoiler alert: If you're a parent, your exhaustion level will always be set to max. You're probably asleep right now. I'm sorry you don't have better dreams.

In a world with books, you quickly grow to hate even the most beloved children's story. Do you really want to hear about the big, hungry bear three thousand times in a row? If you think I'm exaggerating, you're not a parent. These are real-world numbers that everyone who has raised a child can immediately verify. If it were up to me, literary awards for children's books would be given out based solely on brevity. *Goodnight Moon* would sweep every category because it takes thirty seconds to read. When I'm old and can't remember my own name, I'll still have that book embedded in my brain. I've read it so many times, it's not a memory; it's a scar on my soul.

But if the world bans books like in *Fahrenheit 451*, problem solved. True, there will be tragic cultural and sociological issues that crop up throughout your child's life, like lowered creativity and trouble playing Scrabble, but for right now, your kid will go to bed earlier. That means you can go to bed earlier, too. It's worth collapsing civilization for a little extra sleep.

Keep in mind that if you're in a *Fahrenheit 451*–type world, all books are illegal, including this one. I appreciate you risking your life to read my words. Sorry they weren't worth it.

THE LITTLE ENGINE THAT COULD

The Little Engine That Could is a world where trains talk and have attitude problems. Seriously, they're major jerks to each other. They roll right by the train that broke down, offering a litany of excuses for why they can't help: "I'm too important." "I'm running late for Pilates." "I'm hauling nuclear material and by law can't stop due to the risk of a terrorist attack." Full disclosure: It's been a while since I've read the book.

If you and your child get sucked into *The Little Engine That Could*, prepare to walk instead of riding the rails. Even if the trains weren't jerks, I'd be reluctant to let my kid travel on any sentient form of transportation. Horses are bad enough. A train that can think for itself and decide whether or not it wants to go over a mountain? Hard pass. But not a mountain pass. That's the thing the trains refuse to go over.

Not every engine refuses, of course. The Little Blue Engine agrees to help the broken-down engine by hauling its cargo: talking toys intended for the good little girls and boys on the other side of the mountain. If you're a mom or dad, you just shuddered. Talking toys are the bane of parents everywhere, real and fictional. We can't wait till the batteries die or our kids look away so we can cut a few wires and silence their playthings for good. Delivering a trainload of talking toys might seem like a gesture of goodwill, but really it's an act of war. In fact, the parents on the other side of the mountain are the reason the first train broke down. No children's story is complete without a little sabotage.

Even if the Little Blue Engine wasn't hauling a train load of pure evil, it would still teach the wrong lesson to kids. The Little Blue Engine strains until it makes it over the mountain. That shows your kid that if something is too hard, they should keep pushing. Wrong. That's how you get a hernia. A better lesson would be to know your limits and wait for help. Also, don't deliver talking toys to anyone. Leave them on the wrong side of the mountain and bury them there. It will save the lives of countless parents on the other side of the mountain who would have otherwise died from lethal levels of annoyance. Also, if you insist on trying to deliver the toys, the parents from the mountain valley will likely blow the tracks and cause an avalanche, giving you one more thing to survive. That first act of sabotage was just a warning.

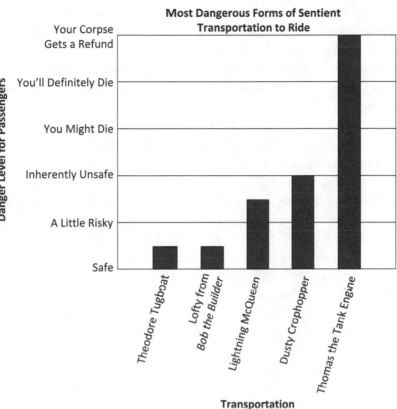

Most Dangerous Forms of Sentient Transportation to Ride

Danger Level for Passengers (y-axis, from bottom to top):
Safe, A Little Risky, Inherently Unsafe, You Might Die, You'll Definitely Die, Your Corpse Gets a Refund

Transportation (x-axis): Theodore Tugboat, Lofty from Bob the Builder, Lightning McQueen, Dusty Crophopper, Thomas the Tank Engine

THE LORD OF THE RINGS

You ask your child why they haven't done their homework yet, and they say it's because they have to go on a quest to throw an evil ring into a volcano. What's a parent to do?

First, tell your kid to hand over the Ring. This is a test. If they hand it over, they're unworthy to protect it and should be playing video games instead. I'd say they should be doing homework, but that's a bigger fantasy than *The Fellowship of the Ring*. For your sake, you better hope your kid doesn't hand over the Ring. It comes with the somewhat noticeable side effect of corrupting your heart and turning you into an unstoppable force of evil. Presumably, your child is immune to the effects of the Ring because your kid possesses a hobbit-like innocence. Either that or they're already so evil that they've reached a saturation point, making any additional corruption moot.

If you do take the Ring, it will ruin your life, unless becoming an unstoppable force of evil is on your bucket list. In that case, congrats on attaining one of your major goals. Remember the little people as you crush them with your armies of darkness.

But if your child refuses to even show you the Ring, try to grab them. If they vanish into thin air, there's a good chance they actually have the One Ring to rule them all. In that case, you likely won't see them again until they complete an epic quest spanning hundreds of miles and many perils. Remind them to take clean underwear.

The discovery of the Ring might give some context to other things your kid has been up to. If they'd previously befriended a group of twelve short, bearded men and suddenly left, only to return months later with a box of treasure and a thousand-yard stare, you'll now understand why. They weren't at a sleepover next door after all. Also, their shifty friend with the tall, pointy hat was exactly as unsavory as you suspected. He does magic, and worse, he smokes. But that elderly vagabond is your child's best chance for survival. Encourage Gandalf to protect your kid. He will if properly compensated. A six-pack should do the trick.

There are some friends you should cut out of your child's life. If nine mysterious figures in black cowls show up at your door, don't let them in, no matter how politely they ask. Also, tell them to get their giant black horses off your lawn. That's a clear violation of homeowners' association rules. If the Ringwraiths want to keep their horses around, they'll have to park them on the street and get a special sticker from the association president. Good luck with that.

If your child didn't disappear for good when you tried to grab them, drive them to the special council where the fate of the Ring will be decided.

Your child might complain that everyone else is showing up on majestic steeds while you're bringing them in a minivan. But the alternative is a perilous journey on foot pursued by evil spirits with swords. Tell your child to quit their whining and buckle up.

At the council, remind the leaders of elves, dwarves, and men that your child has a curfew. All adventures to save Middle-earth must end by 9 PM. For some kids, their curfew is when the streetlights come on, but there are no streetlights in Mordor. Except for that huge, glowing eyeball that can peer an infinite distance in search of the Ring. Keep your curtains closed.

HARRY POTTER

The world of Harry Potter is filled with dangers. I'm talking about the version described in the books and movies, not the version J. K. Rowling retroactively changes on a daily basis to confuse and annoy the internet. By the time my book goes to print, Dumbledore and Grindelwald could have an entire secret family together and the main character of books one through seven might be a frozen treat from Dairy Queen. You're a Blizzard, Harry.

It's impossible to count the number of things in the original world of magic that could kill your kid. Staircases move. Books bite. Adults forget you saved the world multiple times in a row and continue to doubt everything you say. Each of these magical problems has an equally magical solution, and that's not really what this book is about. I've never strayed off topic before, and I'm not going to start now.

If you must save a magical child, tell them to cast *expelliarmus* in every situation and hope for the best. And really, the person most in danger if you have a magical child is you, especially if you're non-magical. Your child would be expelled for using magic outside of Hogwarts, but that wouldn't stop them from turning you into a statue for making them finish their peas. If your child seems magical in any way, send them to live with an awful aunt and uncle. I hear that worked out once before.

If your child isn't magical but is still facing magical dangers, that's more in my wheelhouse. Most of the magical world stays deliberately hidden from Muggles. The only crossover figure, at least in the scope of the original books and movies, is Voldemort, who clearly intends to conquer the magical and non-magical worlds alike. If you aren't magical, you can still fend off Voldemort, but it will take some planning. Band together with the other parents in the neighborhood to draw lightning bolt–shaped scars on all the children's heads. Voldemort will be temporarily paralyzed by self-doubt when he doesn't know who to kill. Or he'll just kill all the children at once. Sometimes, you have to roll the dice, especially with other people's children. As soon as He Who Must Not Be Named shows up, feel free to rub the fake lightning bolt off your kid's head and sneak them out the back.

If all else fails, pretend you've never heard of Voldemort and maybe he'll leave you and the rest of the Muggles alone until he's done battling other wizards. He'll figure subjugating the non-magical folks can wait. Either the wizards will rise to the occasion and stop him, or they won't and the world will be doomed. If it comes to that, you can blame the wizards for failing and wash your hands of the whole matter, even as you're subjected to Voldemort's magic-based class system for the rest of your life. Or maybe just take your kid and immigrate to America. Voldemort had zero interest in crossing the Atlantic Ocean. It's too much of a headache to switch from Celsius to Fahrenheit.

Most Useful Spells for Wizards Raising Kids

Spell	Reason It's Useful
Lumos	Turns on the bathroom light for your kid without you having to get up.
Accio	Gets the remote back once and for all.
Obliviate	Erases your memory so you forget how hard it is to be a parent. Then you'll be ready to have another kid.
Expelliarmus	Makes your toddler put down the hairy candy bar they found in the garbage.
Wingardium Leviosa	Picking up will finally be easy. Your kid still won't do it.
Alohomora	Unlocks doors. Great for when your child "accidentally" locks you out of the house.
Apparate	For when you just need to get out of the house and several hundred miles away.
Expecto Patronum	Scares away Dementors, but will barely slow down your child.

THE SHAWSHANK REDEMPTION

You're probably confused because you saw *The Shawshank Redemption* and it had nothing to do with kids. In this scenario, we're going to say you got locked up unjustly with your child in the cell with you. Why would someone do this? Maybe the law against cruel and unusual punishment was suspended, or perhaps nobody noticed your kid was there and they were locked in with you by accident. Or maybe someone really needed a babysitter and a convicted felon serving a life sentence was the best they could do. As usual, I'm not here to judge you. That job fell to the actual judge. I'm just here to tell you and your kid how to get out.

In the book—and the movie, too, since, let's be honest, that's the only reason 99 percent of us know this story—the wrongly accused man slowly tunnels through the wall of his cell over many years. He hides the hole behind a poster of a beautiful woman. You can still tunnel if your kid is in the cell, but the poster will have to be of Dora the Explorer or the Paw Patrol. Not quite as inspiring, but definitely as effective. No guard will tear that poster off the wall. Leaving it up will be another form of punishment.

Your tunneling will go much faster with two sets of hands. Your child will be elated to destroy a wall with your permission. They would have wrecked your cell anyway, so all you need to do is let them follow their natural instincts. Send your kid ahead to tunnel deeper as you widen the sides. As for disposing of the dirt and rubble, kids love to put that kind of stuff in their pockets. Ideally, your child would dump it out in the prison yard, but they're more likely to hold onto it forever. That's obviously not sustainable. Periodically tip your kid upside down to shake out their pockets. Anybody watching will think this is just a normal incident of a convict disciplining their child in the prison yard as best they know how. Nobody expects you to be a great parent.

When you do finally make a break for it in the middle of a thunderstorm, your child won't have any trouble crawling down the sewer pipe. They will, however, have trouble sitting still in the bank while you withdraw all the cash you hid away as you helped the prison warden launder money. That's okay. Your kid will bolster your cover story. Who would believe an escaped felon would go to the bank with a child throwing a temper tantrum? Nobody. That's why it wasn't in the book.

The hardest part of your escape will be the cross-country road trip to Mexico to live out your days as an escaped fugitive. As you make the multi-day bus ride next to your ornery, fidgety child, you might wish you were back in prison, but this time, alone. You'll consider sending your child on without you as you turn yourself in. Don't. Things will get better once you've assumed a new identity in a new country. And by better, I mean the same, but in a small shack instead of a bus or a prison cell. Then you'll just be an ordinary parent. That's a prison sentence all its own.

CARRIE

Raising a teenager is hard enough when they *can't* start fires with their minds. But take already elevated hormone levels and toss in unexpected pyro-telekinesis and you're in for a rough time. In *Carrie*, Stephen King showed the world what can happen if you pick on the wrong kid, but I suspect the same fire powers are buried somewhere in all of us. (Yes, I know Carrie only caused mayhem that led indirectly to fires, while the girl in *Firestarter* is the one who actually started fires with her mind. But Carrie could start mind fires, too. She just never got around to it because she was too busy dying.) If I were in an extreme situation, like being stuck in a grocery store checkout lane where everyone in front of me paid by check, I might be able to burn down the place with my mind, too. Let's hope we never find out.

Mental fire powers usually cause more problems than they solve, especially if they belong to your child instead of you. If your kid follows the game plan laid out in *Carrie*, their emotions will get the best of them when kids are cruel to them, and they'll burn down a prom. Ah, the awkward teenage years. What do you say to such a kid to make sure they don't do it again, assuming they survived the first one? (And they would survive. Pig's blood has well-known flame-resistant properties.)

Whatever words you choose, say them gently and away from flammable materials. If possible, have this talk in a swimming pool. Your angsty teenager might instead try to use their mind powers to drown you or freeze the water, but you should be safe. Chlorine is equally effective against germs and mind murder.

Then there are the legal ramifications. If your child burns down a gymnasium full of kids, the authorities will get involved. Make sure your child pleads the Fifth. Whether your kid learned their lesson or not, sending them to jail won't help the situation. If your child can transform intense emotions into fire, a prison sentence will lead to crispy inmates, not heartfelt remorse.

Hire an expensive lawyer and your kid has a good chance of beating the charges. How do you prove that somebody committed a crime with their mind? There were no surviving witnesses, and even if there were, they couldn't prove anything. How could a prosecutor pin the fire on your emotional kid rather than all the other emotional kids in the gym? Getting burned alive is kind of a stressful experience. To convict your child, the prosecutor would have to prove the existence of telekinesis and then prove your child and your child alone used their brain waves to do it. Reasonable doubt should be on your child's side. Then again, your child's fate will be determined by twelve people who were too dumb to get out of jury duty. Maybe don't get your hopes up just yet.

Your best bet is to tell your kid to sit patiently through the trial. If they're acquitted, great. They can go on to live a normal life. If they're convicted, they can burn the courtroom and anyone who witnessed the verdict. No prosecutor would volunteer to try them a second time. The truth will set you free, but so will mind fires.

Most Traumatizing Events in a Teenager's Life

Event	Why It's Traumatizing
First Day of High School	Official start of the worst four years of your life.
First Date	Lets someone get close enough to hate the real you.
First Kiss	Gives germs a faster way to merge and mutate.
First Period	Two other periods to get through. Watch out for the Zamboni.
First Time Driving Solo	Did that speed bump just scream?
First Murder Cover-Up	Someone will know what you did last summer.
First Prom	All teenage schemes come to a head.
First After-Prom	Likely held at the morgue or the burn ward.

THE CRUCIBLE

Could witches be real? I guess. I wrote a chapter on how to defend your kid against ghosts and mummies, so anything is possible. But for this section, let's assume witches are imaginary and the real monsters are the witch hunters, like in *The Crucible*. The witches there definitely weren't real. At least I assume not. If it turns out witches existed, then witch-finders have been unfairly defamed and the estate of Arthur Miller is about to get sued.

What should you do if your child is falsely accused of witchcraft? That's harder than if you're falsely accused. In fact, you might secretly hope you are a witch. Just think how great life would be if you could transform annoying neighbors into cows. You would totally abuse that power, if only for the free milk.

But alas, you're neither a witch nor falsely accused of being one. Your child is. You shouldn't be surprised. We all saw this coming. Even at their best, children seem a little satanic. They talk to imaginary friends, pretend to have powers, and throw unholy temper tantrums straight from the pits of hell. Since young kids don't understand the difference between fantasy and reality, it's hard to know when they're having innocent, carefree fun and when they're literally communing with Satan. Most days, it's a toss-up.

If your child is arrested by the witch-finders, tell your kid to be themselves. There's a chance your child will be so awful that the witch-finders will let them go. Does another adult really want to spend enough time in a room with your child to hold a trial, even a fast, unfair one? Time to put that to the test.

If the witch-finders ask your child to name other witches, tell your kid to name farm animals. Who's to say that livestock can't be possessed by the devil? In the Bible, Jesus drives demons out of humans and into pigs. Have your kid tell the witch-finders that all the evil spirits are now in the plumpest hogs. The whole town will have a giant hog roast. Cooking pork to 140 degrees prevents food poisoning and secondhand demons.

If the witch-finders ignore your child's suggestions and instead throw them in the water, tell your kid not to panic. This seems like an impossible scenario. If your child drowns, it proves they were innocent, and if they don't drown, they're a witch. Have your child tell the inquisitors that they're lactose intolerant. When the inquisitors point out that the pond is not, in fact, filled with milk, have your child explain that water is a major component of most dairy products. It's probably the ingredient they were allergic to all along. Have your child offer to drown in a non-water-based alternative, like air. Chances are your child will survive an attempted air drowning, even if they're not very good at holding their breath. Although if they survive, that means they're a witch, so I guess they're right back to square one. Recommend a second air drowning while you think of a better plan. Your kid should be able to survive quite a few of them in a row.

Of course, the easiest way for your child to beat a witch trial is to not be in one in the first place. Before you move anywhere, check the date on the last public witch trial. If it was within the last four hundred years, live someplace else.

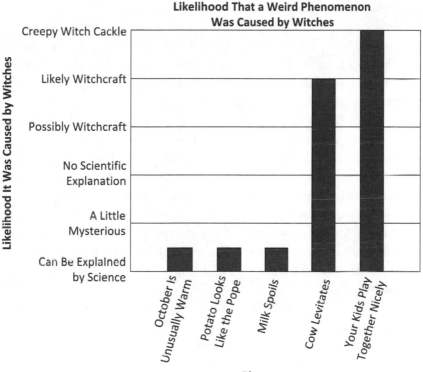

ROMEO AND JULIET

Let's say you find yourself in a modern remake of Shakespeare's *Romeo and Juliet*, but this time you're one of the parents in the story. This is a common predicament, not because the play is a good story, but because the copyright ran out. Lazy writers love to rip off free material.

It's tough living under the rules of Shakespeare's romantic tragedies. Your kid can't love who they want because of local family rivalries. Also, everyone has to talk in iambic pentameter, which is exhausting. Finally, in a world where the outcome for every teenage emotion is death, there's a lot of drama. If Renaissance Verona had had Tinder, everybody would have died.

It's essential that you prevent your child from becoming Romeo or Juliet, whose torrid love affair is Exhibit A for why people should stop looking for a soul mate and just adopt a cat. Juliet was only thirteen, and her three-day romance with Romeo led to the deaths of at least six people. Middle school is the worst.

The easiest way to make sure your child doesn't fall victim to a similar fate is to avoid ancient feuds with rival families. Blood feuds tend to get bloody, which is bad news for everybody, especially the janitor. Vendettas are also time-consuming. It takes so much effort to hate someone else's family that it would be hard to find the energy to hate your own. Pick a different hobby. Racquetball seldom kills anyone.

Even if you eliminate all family feuds, kids create drama on their own, so here's what to do if your child attempts to re-create a *Romeo and Juliet*–style romance anyway. If you're the parent of the younger member of the pair and your child asks if they can marry someone they just met that night, calmly say, "No, you're thirteen." Then ask them if they want their newfound love interest to go to jail. If you have the older member of the pair, spray them with a hose. Will they appreciate this? No. Will it save their life? Probably. Unless they're the Wicked Witch of the West. Then the janitor will have another mess to clean up.

In modern times, you shouldn't care who your child dates as long as they're of legal age and their courtship won't lead to a citywide suicide spree. Give your child some privacy, but also keep an eye out for vials of secret poison. There's no valid reason for anyone to have them before they turn eighteen. Or after they turn eighteen, for that matter. Maybe stores should just stop selling vials of secret poisons. Or at least attach a stronger warning label.

If your child throws a really dramatic fit and then appears to die, don't bury them right away. There's a distinct possibility they faked their death for romantic purposes. Or maybe they're just really upset that you embarrassed them by showing up where their friends could see you. There's nothing more disgraceful than having a parent.

Remind your child that the younger and less educated they are when they marry, the less likely that marriage is to last. Encourage your child to put off their tragically fatal romance until after college. No one should die young. They should get the chance to grow old and die inside a little every day. That's what parenting is all about.

Survival Lessons from Shakespeare's Plays

Play	Survival Lesson
The Taming of the Shrew	Beware of shrew bites.
The Merchant of Venice	Accepted forms of payment include cash, credit, and human flesh.
Henry V	Breaches were made for going into.
Macbeth	Witches give unreliable murder advice.
Hamlet	Ghosts give highly reliable murder advice.
Julius Caesar	Your friends are probably backstabbers.
Richard III	Your enemies are probably front-stabbers.
A Midsummer Night's Dream	Put down the LSD.

MOBY-DICK

Sometimes a white whale isn't really a white whale. It could be anything—a promotion, an award, a love interest—that you pursue to the exclusion of all else, even as that obsession destroys your life. But other times, it literally is a white whale, which is what this section is about. For whatever reason, you and your kid are part of a mission to kill an albino water mammal. Sound unrealistic? Whatever. After reading about werewolf attacks and alien abductions, is this really where you're going to draw the line?

Honestly, there are worse ways to spend quality time with your kid. There are better ones, too. Like nearly every other activity on earth. Hunting a whale together is technically a fishing trip, which means you'll have to wake up early and spend most the day bored out of your mind. Even worse, instead of a fish, you'll be trying to catch a complex, intelligent mammal that only a heartless monster would destroy. But don't worry, it doesn't count as cruel because there's no way you're actually going to kill that whale. If anything, the white whale is on a human-hunting trip. Pray it doesn't bring its kid.

The first step to surviving the quest for the white whale is to figure out who's obsessed with it. If it's the captain and you're just a crew member who will later recount this journey in excruciating, symbol-laden detail, then the odds of you and your kid surviving just went way up. Slack off and stay toward the back during all the dangerous stuff. If the mad captain asks for volunteers to get in his tiny boat to go and stab the giant whale with a pointy stick, don't raise your hand. You'll be much safer on the big boat, especially if you turn it around and sail away as soon as the captain is off the ship. There's no shame in fleeing certain death if it saves your child. In fact, it might even be heroic, especially if you write it up that way in your turgid, overwrought tome.

If it's you who's obsessed with the white whale, you and your child are both at great risk. You'll undoubtedly want your kid at your side as you go in for the kill. Since not being obsessed at that point won't be an option, at least put your kid toward the back of the smaller boat, away from the guy holding the harpoon. Also, make sure your child eats a light lunch so they'll be extra buoyant, and give them a refresher course on how to tread water, because they might be floating in the sea for a very long time. Will any of that stop you from pursuing your own goals at the expense of your child? Of course not. But at least your kid will have plenty of time to think about what a bad parent you were as they tread water for hours or days awaiting rescue. Don't expect a great eulogy at your funeral.

If it's your child who's obsessed with the white whale, you have an even bigger problem. This is all your fault. Why couldn't you get them into a healthier obsession, like basketball or archery boxing? It's like regular boxing, but with crossbows. Thanks to your bad parenting, your child grew up reading anti-whale websites and watching anti-whale cable news. Is there enough demand to support such an oddly specific channel? Probably. I suspect it's run by seals.

Do everything you can to discourage your child from chasing the white whale. Remind them that if they simply don't go in the water, the whale will never bother them again. Also point out that a whale doesn't provide anything they couldn't find on land. Your kid could eat plenty of other animals that are tastier, and oil also comes from the ground. Going out and stabbing a whale from a rowboat is literally the least efficient way to get anything but revenge. And even the revenue angle won't work out because the whale will kill them.

If your child still insists on chasing the white whale, shout, "I see the whale!" Then toss a burlap sack over your kid and drag them back to dry land. Will they hate you forever? Possibly, but at least they'll be alive to do it. In the meantime, the whale will live a full life and eventually die of old age, which will take a very long time. Don't inform your child of this. Instead, tell your kid the whale died from something awful like whale cancer, which, for all your kid knows, could be real. How many whale oncologists do they know? That's what I thought. All lies are justified if they keep your child from pursuing an insane vendetta against a peaceful marine mammal. Words to live by.

THE FINAL CHAPTER

Whether you're sucked into them, imitating them in real life, or simply forced to read them over and over again, books are a special form of torture designed to make your job as a parent as difficult as possible. To survive, you'll need to be vigilant—or maybe just illiterate. Ignorance can save us all.

If you find yourself caught in an absurd parenting scenario that could only exist as the plot of a novel, keep these dos and don'ts in mind:

✓ **Do** be on the lookout for improbable plot twists. When kids are involved, expect randomness at every turn.

✗ **Don't** skip to the end. There's no reason to get to a bad ending faster.

✓ **Do** expect a happy ending. That doesn't mean you'll get one. But if you don't lie to yourself at least a little, you won't get out of bed.

✗ **Don't** expect to understand what's going on. Confusing books are good books, at least according to that English professor you hated.

✓ **Do** look for symbolism. It'll give you something to talk about with your therapist after you fail as a parent.

✗ **Don't** lose your place. Always know where you are, even if it's not where you want to be.

✓ **Do** be the author of your own life. If your parenting experiences are going to turn into a ridiculous story, you might as well be the one collecting royalties.

✗ **Don't** be caught off guard by the sequel. Whether it's another book or another child, it's usually just more of the same, but a little bit worse.

Whether your life is based on a novel or a novel is based on your life, you can get through it with your kid. Remember, when it comes to parenting, you're just a side character. Your child is the chief hero and main villain. Try not to die in their tragic backstory.

CHAPTER 10

VIDEO GAMES

Books aren't the only medium that poses a threat to your kid. Electronic formats arc also out to get you. But if you use them right, they, too, can teach you a valuable lesson about survival. When taken seriously, video games are a training simulation for real life. I don't mean they prepare you to think critically or solve puzzles or persevere against impossible odds. I mean *Donkey Kong* literally teaches you how to save a princess from a giant monkey throwing barrels. In this chapter, I'll tell you how to get your child through the real-world scenarios video games have been preparing you for all along. Hopefully you've been practicing. Screen time saves lives.

And yes, every video game scenario in this chapter could play out in the real world, even if that world isn't necessarily the one you're currently in. In the pantheon of infinite universes that make up reality, it's impossible to deny that, in at least one of them, you and your child might have to dodge L-shaped blocks that fall from the sky. How will you and your child survive? Just like you do everything else as a family: barely. You should be used to it by now.

With a little initiative and a few cheat codes, you can raise a child in a 2D world just as effectively as you can in a 3D one. And if you fail, well, your kid will probably have multiple lives, so you'll have more than one chance to get it right. Just don't rely on respawning too much. I'd hate for you to miss the last checkpoint and have to redo your child's terrible twos.

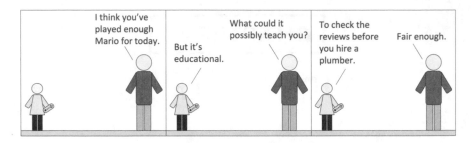

CRUIS'N USA

A cross-country road race like the one in the N64 classic *Cruis'n USA* is perilous enough on its own. Now add in a child and slam down the gas. Here comes the worst road trip of your life.

During a normal car trip with a child, you have to stop for a bathroom break approximately every four miles depending on how old your kid is and how many gallons of orange juice they drank. In an illegal road race across the country, those frequent stops won't be an option—at least not if you want to win, instead of taking a scenic tour of every rest stop in America. To stay on the road, train your child to use a bottle. This may require some accessories, like a funnel, but it should be doable. Of course, then you'll have to ask yourself if the glory of winning is worth having the smell of human urine in your car for a thousand miles. I'm going with "no."

Alternatively, you could convince your child to drink less. That should be easy if you don't bring any liquids in your car in the first place. Of course, if you don't hyper-hydrate your kid, you'll have to listen to them complain about how they're thirsty across sixteen states. You'll probably end up giving them something to drink and gritting your teeth through the resulting ninety-seven bathroom breaks. At least you'll have a chance to go, too.

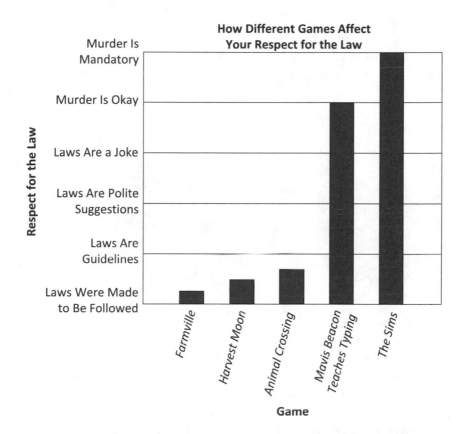

How Different Games Affect Your Respect for the Law

Respect for the Law (y-axis, top to bottom): Murder Is Mandatory, Murder Is Okay, Laws Are a Joke, Laws Are Polite Suggestions, Laws Are Guidelines, Laws Were Made to Be Followed

Game (x-axis): Farmville, Harvest Moon, Animal Crossing, Mavis Beacon Teaches Typing, The Sims

Since you'll be at a disadvantage by taking your child on this road trip, you'll have to drive dirty to gain ground. Ram other vehicles off the road. This might seem unethical, but the other cars have insurance, which makes it okay. Just make sure you and your kid have your seat belts fastened and your barf bags ready first. Your car is going to do some major flipping. You're not really driving until you're airborne.

If you properly manage your car's speed and your child's bladder, you could win the ultimate prize: a huge trophy that means nothing. You'll also get a highly abbreviated view of the country. According to the game's total play time, it only takes about twenty minutes to drive across the United States. It's a wonder anybody flies. After completing a race across this beautiful if abridged scenery, your child will finally appreciate what makes this country great: taking unnecessary risks for a long-shot chance at fleeting glory. God bless America.

DONKEY KONG

Nothing makes a day go from bad to worse like a giant barrel-throwing gorilla stealing your child for reasons that are his own. Nobody knows why Donkey Kong wants your kid. Back when he stuck to stealing princesses, he never ate them or married them. Maybe he just wants some company but lacks the social skills to make friends. Whatever. You're a parent, not an ape therapist. Just kick his butt and get your kid back.

Donkey Kong takes all of his captives to the top floor of a construction site, where he has a suspiciously large supply of wooden barrels to throw at you. Where do these barrels come from? The only thing stored in wooden barrels these days is whiskey. Donkey Kong must have a drinking problem, which explains his erratic behavior. Don't let him hit you with his empties.

When Donkey Kong hurls his barrels, they roll down steel girders and block your path. Don't try to jump them. Your knees can't take the impact. At your current age, simply sneezing can throw out your back. Instead, look for an elevator. If the building doesn't have one, sue the owner. Then they'll be forced to add an elevator shaft, and maybe they'll deal with the giant child-stealing gorilla on the roof at the same time. The whole situation is definitely a violation of public accommodation laws. A building with a massive primate throwing barrels down a ramp is in no way handicap accessible.

If the litigation is moving too slowly to save your child in a timely fashion, hide inside an empty barrel that Donkey Kong already threw. At some point, he must reuse them. He can't afford that many new barrels on a gorilla's salary. When his barrel retrieval service delivers you to the top floor, pull your kid into the barrel with you, then roll down the girders to safety. Donkey Kong will be too drunk to pursue you. That's why he just stays in one spot and throws things at people. He's truly living the dream.

GOLDENEYE 007

If you somehow end up raising a child in a universe exactly like the first-person shooter *GoldenEye 007* on N64, use your kid to your advantage. In the game, it's a pain to point guns up or down, so most people shoot straight ahead at chest level. Your short child can walk under that hail of bullets, making them even more unstoppable than Odd Job. Unless your kid is a full-grown teenager, in which case tell them to duck. That's good life advice for any situation.

Really, parenting inside *GoldenEye 007* won't be that different than parenting anywhere else. In the game, as in real life, hiding in the bathroom is always the best move. Whether you need a good cry or just want to set up a defensive position to gun down Russian soldiers, the bathroom is your fortress of solitude. Never yield it to someone else. Of course, in the real world, you would lock your child out of the bathroom rather than inside with you. To keep your kid safe in the virtual world, stuff them in the bathroom's air vents, which are impervious to nearly all nonexplosive attacks. Note: Before you attempt this, make absolutely certain that you are, in fact, in a video game world where your child is in mortal peril. That will determine whether you get a visit from a child welfare caseworker or the man with the golden gun.

If possible, arm your kid with proximity mines. These are bombs that stick to walls and explode if approached by enemies—or friends. Your child naturally sticks things to other things anyway. That's why every surface in your house is covered with stickers, boogers, and candy residue impervious to both cleaning solutions and fire. If there's a surface of your house that isn't sticky, it must be new. In your child's hands, proximity mines will soon be stuck to everything, obliterating your enemies. Just make sure you don't intend to go anywhere else on that level again.

At least getting stuck with your kid in *GoldenEye 007* is a great chance to teach your child culture. Take your child to the Temple, where they can learn that Egyptians had giant, empty tombs with automatic doors. Or take them to the Library, which contains no actual books. That seems oddly prophetic now that many libraries are just publicly funded computer labs. Of course, the Library in *GoldenEye 007* doesn't have computers either, just catwalks and, if you choose the right setting, grenade launchers. Those are also excellent educational tools, but only for teaching your kid about how fun it is to make things go boom.

Even better, your kid will be easier to track in the *Goldeneye 007* world than they are in this one. Everybody moves at the same frustratingly slow speed, unless they move diagonally, which somehow bends space and time to make them travel faster. Plus there's radar. In real life, you don't have that luxury, unless you install a tracking app on your kid's phone. I promise that's not cheating. Neither is camping.

Overall, caring for your child in the *GoldenEye 007* universe should be a rich and fulfilling experience. As long as you and your child don't die from the literally thousands of bullets flying at you at all times, it's a great place to raise a kid.

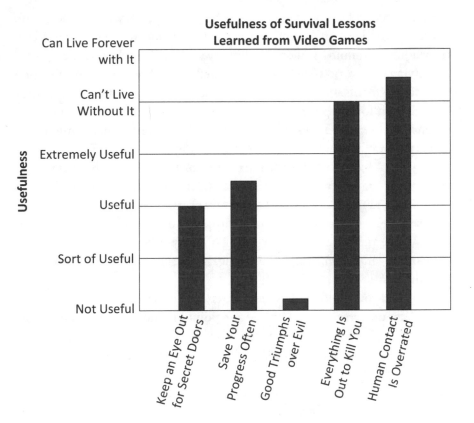

GRAND THEFT AUTO

Raising a kid in a world like Grand Theft Auto shouldn't be too hard since it's basically the universe we live in now, only more intense. People there steal cars as casually as we call Ubers; their fender benders result in catastrophic explosions rather than just erupting tempers; and their running gun battles happen in public spaces a few times a day rather than just a few times a week. It's essentially a day in our normal world if everyone forgot to drink their coffee. But there's a major positive of the Grand Theft Auto world: Traffic laws are optional. You'll get your kid to soccer practice in record time, assuming you don't get hit by a rocket launcher on the way.

Living in a world based on Grand Theft Auto should also cut down on your car payments. Just walk up to someone, steal their exotic ride, and hide long enough for the police to lose interest, which should take about thirty seconds, as long as you don't kill anyone in the process. Murder might add an extra minute or two. After that, you'll legally own the car for life. Guess what your kid is getting for their sixteenth birthday. The only downside is someone could just as easily steal a car from your child. Tell your kid to buckle up and never open the door for strangers. If you and your kid do get hijacked, politely ask the carjacker to drop you off at your original destination. Maybe the carjacker will let you both stay in the car so they can use the carpool lane. Crime might be wrong, but it can still be environmentally friendly.

You and your child will have an entirely different worldview in the Grand Theft Auto universe. There won't be any point in sending your kid to school so they can get a nine-to-five job when all they need to succeed is a gun and a total lack of morality. Crime pays, and very well. Tell your child they can live a rich and fulfilling life as long as they always have the bigger weapon. Also, make sure your kid stays in good shape because they'll be running away a lot. The entire justice system is based on staying slightly out of sight until the cops get bored. All things considered, that's roughly as fair as the system we have today. Why dispense justice based on who can afford the best lawyer when you could base it on a high-stakes game of hide-and-seek?

Top Things Stolen in Video Games

What's Stolen	Why It's Wrong
Gold Coins	Doesn't matter if you found them on the ground. They're still not yours.
Princesses	There's a reason people used to lock them in towers.
Magic Weapons That Can Destroy the Earth	The Second Amendment doesn't apply if you can blow up the world.
Boxes and Chests	Go ahead and break them open to see what's inside. I'm sure the rightful owners won't mind.
Pokémon	You're stealing them from nature.
Special Moves	Imitation is the sincerest form of flattery—and murder.
Anything on a Corpse	Respect the dead. You never know when they'll come back and try to eat you.
Precious Hours of Your Life You've Wasted Playing Video Games	You're never getting those back.

HALO

In the Halo universe, a cybernetic super-soldier battles aliens who believe an ancient ring world will send them all to alien heaven. In reality, the ring kills all life to stop space zombies from spreading. Is that really a good environment in which to raise a kid? Meh. It's no worse than Florida.

If you find yourself caring for a child on a ring world in the middle of a religious space war, take some basic safety precautions. Lock your doors at night, and never approach strange aliens who are dual-wielding plasma rifles. Keep your kid home in case of rain or orbital bombardments. And if the ring world starts to rumble like it's about to explode, move. Always keep your minivan gassed up.

To help keep your kid alive in the middle of religious space wars, always keep them up to date on the latest technology, whether it's the newest phone or cybernetic body armor that turns your child into an unstoppable death machine. Thanks to their superior robotic strength, they will be able to open even the most stubborn jar. Spaghetti with cut-up hot dogs will never be late again—or else. Find some cybernetic armor for yourself to restore the balance of power. As a bonus, you'll be shielded from any biohazards during diaper changes. Are those strong, robotic fingers sensitive enough to wipe a baby's butt? You're about to find out.

Raising your kid on a ring world under attack by evil aliens will also teach your child a valuable lesson about organized religion. Faith is good when it encourages acts of charity but not so much when it promotes wiping out all life in the galaxy. Always read the whole pamphlet before converting.

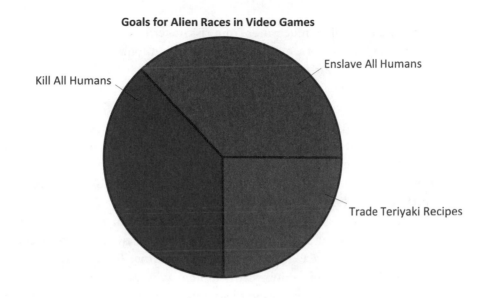

Goals for Alien Races in Video Games

Kill All Humans

Enslave All Humans

Trade Teriyaki Recipes

MADDEN

Your child seems different today. They walk a little taller and sit a little straighter. Also, they suddenly have freakish football abilities that let them score ninety-six points in three quarters. Must have been something they ate. Or maybe you were both sucked inside a virtual sports simulation, where your child is the perfect pro. Occam's razor need not apply. Unfortunately, every other player in the league can also score ninety-six points per game. Welcome to Madden, the most popular football video game in the world. Tell your child to keep their blocks high and their hopes low. This is going to hurt.

The good news is your child doesn't need to fear lingering injuries. They can collide with the other team game after game without any long-term brain damage. In that respect, being sucked into a video game is far safer than playing sports in real life. Instead of signing up your kid for football next fall, maybe just hand them a controller and see if the Xbox eats them.

Your child will be much more of a risk-taker in the Madden universe, but the good news is it won't matter. Go for it on fourth down? Why not? Hail Mary from your own 2-yard line? Absolutely. Punting? What's that? The more unlikely a play is to work, the more likely your child is to try it. Children have a poor understanding of consequences, which makes them almost exactly like real-world professional athletes. But inside Madden games, the consequences your child faces are limited to the field. They don't include getting cut in the locker room, humiliated at the press conference, or busted at the nightclub. It's for the best. The game developers didn't have time to add in a legal simulator.

The biggest risk to your child in the Madden universe is that their accomplishments will lose all sense of meaning. When Super Bowls come easy, what else is there to achieve? Literally anything. Teach your child not to define themselves by arbitrary athletic achievements that people will forget about as soon as the next sports season rolls around. Or maybe just teach your kid to also dominate at FIFA.

Sports That Are Better as Video Games

Sport	Why It's Better as a Video Game
Soccer	Somebody actually scores.
Hunting	Less cleanup. Fewer protesters.
Bowling	You don't come home smelling like secondhand smoke.

Mixed Martial Arts	Fighters never get busted for steroids, and everybody makes weight.
Hockey	You lose fewer teeth.
Darts	Fewer trips to the emergency room.
Car Racing	Easier to walk away from a fatal crash.
Tennis	Other people can't hear you grunt.

MARIO WORLD

You bend over to wipe your kid during a traumatic bathroom visit when you both fall in the toilet. You come out the other side into a pixelated world filled with Goombas slowly pacing back and forth. Why are they so restless? They're probably tweaking. When magic mushrooms randomly fall out of boxes, there are bound to be consequences.

All Goombas have to do to kill you is run into you. But inexplicably, these tiny creatures of instant death die if you jump on top of them. This is good news. If there's one thing your kid likes to do, it's jump on things they shouldn't, like beds, couches, breakable toys, and you, if you make the mistake of lying down. Let your kid take point. If you see something, tell your child to jump on it. Best-case scenario, it dies. Worst-case scenario, nothing happens. Unless your kid jumps down a bottomless pit. It's not the fall that kills you. It's starvation.

Living in Mario World will require you to reverse some of your previous safety standards. When you see a strange mushroom on the ground, tell your child to eat it. Under normal circumstances, this could lead to indigestion or even death. But in Mario World, the worst thing that will happen is that your child will become a temporary giant. Luckily, their clothes will grow with them, rather than just exploding. Otherwise, your wardrobe costs would skyrocket. The only thing more inconvenient than a growth spurt is a growth spurt that reverses itself the first time you take damage.

Other mushrooms can give your child another life. This would seem to have deep philosophical and religious implications, but it doesn't. Adding extra lives, up to a maximum of ninety-nine, just gives your child more chances to jump on things. What more could you want from incremental immortality?

Not all plants are good for your kid. Don't let your child eat the fire flower. If you think they're hard to deal with now, just wait until your kid can shoot fire from their hands. At least they won't have to wash them. Fire sanitizes all.

The worst thing about this new world will be that your child will want to save a princess or prince. (Yes, I know the kidnapped victim is usually a princess, but progressive, empowered kidnappers don't discriminate along gender lines. Welcome to whatever year you're currently reading this in.) A child chasing after a kidnapped member of the royal family creates an unhealthy relationship dynamic, especially if the only thing they catch is feelings. Rather than growing and changing together, your kid will always be pursuing their love interest, who will inexplicably be locked away inside yet another evil castle. Mushroom Kingdom royalty are too good for bodyguards or basic self-defense. If you have a teenager, at least the constant royal kidnappings will reduce their risk of an unplanned pregnancy by limiting their alone time with their crush. Bowser is the ultimate birth control.

Accompany your child on any rescue mission. That way, you can protect them from death or dismemberment while chaperoning the date. Try not to get in harm's way yourself. Bowser's castle is decorated with spikes and lava, so the place isn't exactly childproof. Bring Band-Aids and burn ointment. With luck, your child will reach the prince or princess and have a chaste, closely supervised reunion. And if not, you'll both die trying. Hopefully your kid saved a few green mushrooms for you.

MORTAL KOMBAT

Every kid needs a hobby. Maybe they'll take up soccer or ballet, or perhaps they'll fight to the death using slick hand-to-hand combat moves and occasional magic in a tournament to determine the greatest warrior of all time. That's Mortal Kombat in a nutshell, and from this moment forward, let's assume you live in a universe where the tournament is real. Your kid will try to enter, even if they're not old enough. Some of the fighters will be millennia-old demigods, so your grade schooler will be at a slight disadvantage. You'll have to sign a permission slip. Don't. The easiest way to keep your kid alive is to keep them out of magic mixed martial arts battles. That's Parenting 101.

But let's say your child fakes your signature and enters the tournament anyway. After all, they're planning to beat other humans to death for sport. Do you really think they're above forgery? Clearly, you haven't done the best job of raising them, but it's never too late to start. Give them the lifesaving assistance they need to win the tournament, or at least survive it. It's time to fight dirty.

At the start of each round, tell your child to bow politely to their opponent as you come up from behind and hit their opponent with your car. The rules of Mortal Kombat don't specifically forbid vehicular intervention. Then drive away before anybody can stop you. Your child will be impressed by your bold decision making. And if they're not, take them out for pizza. They'll soon forget all about their quest for everlasting Kombat glory.

If it's not possible to bring your vehicle into the fight, coach your child as the match goes on. Stick to practical advice. "Stop getting punched in the face." "Stop bleeding." "You're dead. Shake it off." If that doesn't work, toss your child random items, like folding chairs or flamethrowers. Some of the fighters can shoot lightning from their fingertips, so you're just leveling the playing field. And their opponent. And half of the dojo.

Afterward, it's important to talk to your child about why everything they did was morally reprehensible. Unless they made a bunch of money.

Then whatever they did was justified, and you should book another fight as soon as possible. It's the right thing to do.

TETRIS

There are giant blocks falling from the sky, threatening to smash you and everyone you love. For once, the weatherman was right.

It might seem weird to live in the *Tetris* universe, but it's not that different from the world you live in right now. In your current situation, problems seem to fall from the sky, and you have to make everything in your life line up to get rid of them. But in another, more literal way, the normal world isn't anything like the *Tetris* one. Have you ever had a falling brick crash through your ceiling? It's a reality only a roofer could love.

To keep your child safe in a world where blocks fall from the sky, keep your kid on the move. Plan ahead and stack blocks as best you can, keeping your child out of the way. You should be awesome at this. It's basically one big game of cleanup, just like in the normal world, where you put everything exactly where it goes as your kid moves faster and faster to get it back out. Of course, in the end, the mess always wins. Chaos rules all.

You can't stop the advance of anarchy, but you can slow it down a little. With careful planning, you can briefly keep up with life's problems and solve them line by line. But there will always be that one weird block you don't expect, and it'll mess up everything. This sudden intrusion is the same in the regular and block worlds. As a parent, you should be prepared for it, and by "prepared," I mean you can't do anything about it, so get ready to swear. The secret to *Tetris* is you never beat it. It just keeps getting harder and harder until you lose. Embrace the futility and you're sure to succeed until you fail. As a parent, it's the best you can do.

GAME OVER

Some scientists believe our universe may be nothing more than a digital simulation on an alien supercomputer. If that's true, who's to say universes based on video games can't be just as real as our own? Perhaps the rules in our "real" world are just as strange, contrived, and divorced from the reality of our supercomputer overlords as the rules of *Tetris* are from ours. We can only do the best we can where we are, whether we're in a world where we grow up, get jobs, and pay taxes, or one where Italian plumbers shoot fireballs. There goes the smoke detector again.

Remember, your life and your child's life do matter, even if you're in a universe where you can use up those lives like tissues. The rules may change, but your duty to keep your child safe remains constant. As you protect them, keep these dos and don'ts in mind:

✘ **Don't** increase the difficulty setting. Parenting in easy mode is hard enough.

✓ **Do** work together with your kid. Friendly fire will only cost you points.

✗ **Don't** get distracted by side quests. Of your 10,282 daily duties, the most important one is to help your child survive.

✓ **Do** hoard health packs. Health care is expensive. Take all the free perks you can get.

✗ **Don't** judge yourself by normal-world parenting standards. Nobody cares that your kid is valedictorian if their school is crushed by falling bricks.

✓ **Do** tell your child you love them all the time. You never know when they'll move on to the next level without you.

✗ **Don't** worry about ecological repercussions. Nature will be just fine even if your kid stomps every single turtle they see.

✓ **Do** have fun. What's the point in helping your child barely escape death over and over again if you can't enjoy it?

With those pointers in mind, you and your child should be fine in any video game environment. Just don't try to climb the leaderboards. There's no hall of fame for parenting.

CHAPTER 11

THE FINAL CHALLENGE

After reading this book, you're prepared to raise your child in every extreme, convoluted, deadly situation ever conceived—except for one. That last environment is so complex, dangerous, and unpredictable there's no way to prepare for it. You know the one, even if you don't want to admit it. I'm talking, of course, about ordinary life.

On most days, you won't be tossed back in time or sucked into an alternate universe based on a video game or attacked by a goose. Life is a lot harder when your biggest challenge is getting your kid out the door on time so they catch the bus. You won't have a surge of adrenaline from your fight-or-flight response. You'll just have to grind it out day after day against the same unchanging, unrelenting burdens—with only the occasional alien invasion or teen telekinetic firestarter thrown in. Real life is the real challenge. This is where your mental, physical, and spiritual being will be tested to their utmost. Can you rise to the task of raising your child on an ordinary day in your ordinary life? If you can, every other challenge in this book will pale in comparison. And if you can't, well, you're in for a rough eighteen years.

Does that mean you shouldn't have bought this book? No. I needed the money. But more importantly (as if anything could be more important than paying me), it's good to give yourself some reassurance that when your kid gets waylaid by pirates or Cylons or monsters under the bed, you'll know what to do. Just combine the specific advice in this book with everything you've learned through the extreme challenges of your day-to-day life as a parent. And if all that fails, throw this book at your attacker and run away. Maybe it will distract them. And then buy a replacement copy because, hey, I have to eat.

ACKNOWLEDGMENTS

This list of people I'd like to thank looks pretty familiar. Apparently the same individuals have stood by me through all three books. Either that or I just keep copying and pasting the same list because I'm too lazy to think of new names. Pick whichever interpretation puts the following people in a better light:

- My literary agent, Mark Gottlieb of Trident Media Group. You continue to find homes for my books, both here and abroad. Thanks for making my bad ideas international.
- Glenn Yeffeth, publisher of BenBella Books. This is the third book you've published with me. I can only conclude you never got around to reading the first two. Thanks for being too busy to perform due diligence.
- Leah Wilson, BenBella Editor-in-Chief. Remember when all the other BenBella editors passed on my first book and you got stuck editing it by default? Just think of how many weird conversations about day-care zombies, strategic laziness, and T-rex arm wrestling you almost missed out on. I'm infinitely grateful you were too polite to turn down that first book—and the ones that came after it.
- My kids. Thanks for staying alive. If one of you had died in a rogue ostrich attack, it really would have put a damper on this book.
- My wife. Your patience is legendary. My next book should be a wife's guide to surviving me.

ABOUT THE AUTHOR

Photo by David Van Deman

James Breakwell is a professional comedy writer and amateur father of four girls, ages nine and under. He is best known for his family humor Twitter account, @XplodingUnicorn, which boasts more than one million followers and has been featured on media outlets around the world.

James's first book, *Only Dead on the Inside: A Parent's Guide to Surviving the Zombie Apocalypse*, has saved thousands of lives. To date, not a single person who's read it has died in a zombie attack. But if you do die, James will give you a refund. Offer null and void if you try to bite him.

James's second book, *Bare Minimum Parenting: The Ultimate Guide to Not Quite Ruining Your Child*, taught regular moms and dads to best overachieving parents by doing less. The book started out as a joke but accidentally proved a real point and helped real parents in the process. James is still pretty upset about it.

His guided journal for kids, *Prance Like No One's Watching: How to Live Like an Exploding Unicorn*, is scheduled for release in early 2020.

Keep track of James's ongoing failings as a father and a human being at ExplodingUnicorn.com or on any of the following platforms:

- /ExplodingUnicorn
- /james_breakwell
- /jamesbreakwell
- /xplodingunicorn

This isn't a book about overachieving at parenting.
This isn't even a book about achieving exactly the right amount.

THIS IS A BOOK ABOUT DOING AS LITTLE AS POSSIBLE WITHOUT QUITE RUINING YOUR CHILD.

Available where books are sold.

ExplodingUnicorn.com